Teach Yourself Accents
North America

Teach Yourself Accents North America

A Handbook for Young Actors and Speakers

Robert Blumenfeld

An Imprint of Hal Leonard Corporation

Published in 2013 by Limelight Editions
An Imprint of Hal Leonard Corporation
7777 West Bluemound Road
Milwaukee, WI 53213

Trade Book Division Editorial Offices
33 Plymouth St., Montclair, NJ 07042

Printed in the United States of America

Book design by Mark Lerner

Library of Congress Cataloging-in-Publication Data

Blumenfeld, Robert.
 Teach yourself accents -- North America : a handbook for young actors and speakers / Robert Blumenfeld.
     pages cm. -- (Teach yourself accents)
 Includes bibliographical references.
 ISBN 978-0-87910-808-3
 1. Acting. 2. English language--Dialects--English-speaking countries--Handbooks, manuals, etc. I. Title.
 PN2071.F6B483 2013
 792'.028--dc23
                                    2013018026

www.limelighteditions.com

With gratitude and inexpressible love to my wonderful,
sweet, brilliant parents, Max David Blumenfeld (1911–1994)
and Ruth Blumenfeld (b. 1915)

CONTENTS

ACKNOWLEDGMENTS

I would like to thank my many language teachers at Princeton High School and at Rutgers and Columbia Universities. I extend thanks, also, to the staff of the Stella Adler Conservatory; to Mr. Albert Schoemann, Ms. Pamela Hare, and Mr. Mark Zeller at the once-flourishing National Shakespeare Conservatory; and to my students at both those schools. Very special thanks are due to my wonderful friend Mr. Christopher Buck for his love and support, always. I want to express my thanks and gratitude to my friend Mr. Derek Tague for his special contribution in lending me rare books on accents; and to Bryan Trenis for information on Southern accents. I would also like to thank my very dear and beloved friends for their unfailing love and support over the many years we have known one another: Mr. Albert S. Bennett; Mr. Gannon McHale, distinguished actor; Tom and Virginia Smith; Peter Subers and Rob Bauer; Kieran Mulcare and Daniel Vosovic; Michael Mendiola and Scot Anderson; James Mills; and my family: Nina Koenigsberg, my cousins' cousin; my brother Donald Blumenfeld-Jones, my sister-in-law Kathryn Corbeau Blumenfeld-Jones, and their children, Rebecca and Benjamin; my maternal aunt Mrs. Bertha Friedman (1913–2001), and my cousin, her daughter Marjorie Loewer; my maternal uncle, Seymour "Sy" Korn (1920–2010); my paternal cousin, Jonathan Blumenfeld; and my wonderful maternal grandparents from Galicia in the Austro-Hungarian Empire, Morris Korn (1886–1979) and Harriet Korn (1886–1980). I owe a great debt to the authors of the books listed in the Selected Bibliography, without whose work this book would have been impossible.

I especially want to thank Lon Davis, whose wonderful copy editing of my manuscript has been invaluable; my indefatigable editor, Ms. Jessica Burr, whose dedication and hard work have been wonderful; and my publisher, Mr. John Cerullo, always an encouraging and forthright friend. Special thanks are due to Mr. Mel Zerman (1931–2010), founder and publisher of Limelight Editions, who was not only very helpful throughout the process of getting my first book, *Accents: A Manual for Actors*, published by Limelight in 1998, but was also a kind, charming, and erudite man, one who is greatly missed.

LIST OF PHONETIC SYMBOLS USED IN THIS BOOK

Vowels and Semi-Vowels

ah: like "a" in *father*

a: like "a" in *that*

aw: like "aw" in *law*

ee: like "ee" in *meet*

e: like "e" in *met*

é: a pure vowel similar to the diphthong "ay"; heard in French; lips close together

ih: like "i" in *bit*

ih: a vowel intermediate between /ih/ and /ee/, pronounced with the mouth closed more than for /ih/ and open wider than for /ee/; used in some Hispanic accents in English, where /ih/ does not exist

o: like "o" in *not*

o: like "o" in *work*

oo: like "oo" in *book*; spelled "u" in *pull*

ooh: like "oo" in *boot*

u: like the "u" in *but*

ü: the German umlauted "u" and the French vowel spelled "u" in French; pronounced by saying /ee/ with the lips well protruded, as for /ooh/; heard in some Scottish pronunciations

uh: the schwa; the sound of "e" in *the* before a consonant: *the story* y: the semi-vowel spelled "y" in *yes*

w: the semi-vowel spelled "w" in *wear* and *we* and "o" in *one*

Diphthongs

ay: the diphthong composed of /e/, which is the stressed half of the diphthong, and /ee/; spelled "ay" in *say*

I: the diphthong composed of /ah/, which is the stressed half of the diphthong, and /ee/; spelled "i" in *fight*

oh: the diphthong composed of /u/, which is the stressed half of the diphthong, and /ooh/ in American English; of the schwa /uh/ and /ooh/ in
British English; spelled "o" in *home*

ow: the diphthong composed of /a/, which is the stressed half of the diphthong, and /ooh/; spelled "ow" in *how* and "ou" in *house*

oy: the diphthong composed of /aw/, which is the stressed half of the
diphthong, and /ee/; spelled "oy" in *boy*

yooh: the diphthong composed of the semi-vowel /y/ and the vowel /ooh/,
which is the stressed half of the diphthong; spelled *you*. This diphthong
is the name of the letter "u" in the English alphabet.

Consonants

The consonants /b/, /d/, /f/, /g/ as in *get*, /k/, /h/, /l/, /m/, /n/, /p/, /r/, /s/,
/t/, /v/, and /z/ have the standard phonetic values of General American
English or British RP. The following additional symbols are used:

ch: like "ch" in *church*; a combination of the sounds /t/ and /sh/

j: like "dg" in *edge* or "j" in *just*

kh: like "ch" in Scottish *loch*; a guttural consonant in Arabic, Hebrew, Yiddish, and German

ng: like "ng" in *thing*

nk: like "nk" in *think*

sh: like "sh" in *show*

th: voiced, as in *this*

th: voiceless, as in *thing*

ts: like "ts" in *sets*

zh: like "s" in *measure, pleasure*

?: glottal stop, which replaces the sound of /t/ in certain words in some accents

Pronunciations are enclosed in forward slash marks: / /.

Stressed syllables in pronunciations are in capital letters.

Introduction
Teach Yourself Accents: The Elements

What Is an Accent?

An accent is a systematic pattern of pronunciation: the prototypical, inseparable combination of sounds, rhythm, and intonation with which a language is spoken. Nearly everyone who grows up in a specific region and social milieu pronounces the language in a similar way, so we can usually tell from someone's accent where that person is from, and to what socioeconomic class an individual belongs.

In show business, we use the words *accent* and *dialect* interchangeably, as in the title "dialect coach" for someone who teaches accents to actors, but, technically, they are not the same thing. A dialect is a complete version or variety of a language, with its grammar and vocabulary, as well as the particular accent or accents with which it is spoken.

Like every language, English has its dialects, including those known as Standard British English and Standard American English. Although mutually comprehensible, these dialects are dissimilar in many ways: An English person is "meant" to do something; an American is "supposed" to do it. In London, people live in flats; in New York, they live in apartments. An English person who wants to visit you may "knock you up," but don't say that to an American! As George Bernard Shaw quipped, "England and America are two countries separated by a common language." Then there are Standard Scottish English (SSE), Australian English (AusE), and many other varieties, each with its own accents, idioms, and colorful slang. In Sydney, if you're thirsty, you might want to whip over on the knocker (immediately) to the bottle-shop (liquor store) for some cold tinnies of amber (beer). But in Glasgow you would go to an *offie*, a shortening of the U.K. term "off license," a store where you buy alcoholic beverages to be consumed off the premises. Go get a carry-out before the offie shuts!

There are two kinds of accents: those native to a language, and foreign accents, used by people with a different mother tongue who have learned a language. The two principal standard native accents of English—markedly different from each other—are known as British RP ("Received Pronunciation"), the accent with which Standard British English is spoken; and General American, the most widely used accent of Standard American English.

The muscular habits you have learned automatically and unconsciously—the way you form and utter sounds using the lips, tongue, and resonating chamber that is the inside of the mouth—are so ingrained that it is often difficult to learn the new muscular habits required when you learn another language. Sounds that are similar in the new language to the sounds you already know are, therefore, formed using the old habits. And there are always sounds in the new language that do not exist in the old, and that some people have great difficulty learning to pronounce correctly, such as the /th / *th*/ sounds of English. These are two of the factors that account for the existence of a foreign accent, easily heard as foreign by native speakers. There are also people who learn to speak English or any other language with virtually no discernible foreign accent.

If you are going to do a foreign accent, it's essential to learn some of the language. You will then have a feeling for the muscular habits, for how the lips and tongue are positioned and used during speech. And you will use this basic positioning or placement of the muscles when speaking English. This will automatically give you at least the beginning of the accent. Sometimes this general positioning is all that is required, perhaps with a couple of specific vowel or consonant sounds added to it.

Native accents include a widely accepted, standard, non-regional accent alongside regional pronunciations. You unconsciously learn your accent from the people you go to school with and who surround you, even more than you do from your parents. If your parents speak with a foreign accent, for instance, you will nevertheless speak with the native accent that you hear constantly, at least if you have been born in a place, or arrived there when you were not yet twelve.

Accents, like languages, disappear when the last speaker dies. There are now only a relatively few upper-class Americans who speak as President Franklin D. Roosevelt did in 1941. The British accents recorded on Edison's wax cylinders by Florence Nightingale; by the poet Alfred, Lord Tennyson; and by actors of the late Victorian period, performing the works of Gilbert and Sullivan, no longer exist. And the native New York City accents of the 1920s and 1930s, preserved in films of the period, such as *Dead End* (1937), are largely a thing of the past, though still well remembered, but the American stage diction of the late nineteenth century as recorded by Edwin Booth in 1890 is something nobody now recalls, and it is different from the recorded British stage diction of the same period. Should you need to use one of these historic accents, you have ample recorded material to listen to.

Whether foreign or native, every accent contains four elements, each of which can be studied separately, but all of which work together simultaneously to form the accent:

1. General positioning, placement, and use of the mouth muscles (lips, tongue) during speech;
2. Rhythm, determined by stress patterns;
3. Music, determined by pitch and intonation patterns;
4. Phonetics, the specific sounds of vowels and consonants, the nature of those sounds being conditioned by the positioning of the mouth muscles, which differs—however slightly—from accent to accent.

Begin your work by reading the summary of the most important information about the accent, and by seeing how it differs from yours, comparing its features with those of your own accent. How do you naturally speak? How do use the muscles of the mouth when you speak? How does this use differ when you do an accent?

Your goal as an actor is to internalize and assimilate the accent so that it becomes your natural, habitual way of speaking, so that it is simply part of you, and not put on. The one exception is when the character is deliberately pretending to be someone with an accent, often a bad, comical one that they intend to be convincing, like several Viennese characters posing as either French or Hungarian aristocrats in Johann Strauss's operetta *Die Fledermaus* (The Bat).

How the Muscles of the Mouth Are Used

The first thing to study when learning an accent is the way the muscles of the mouth are used when you speak. The musculature of the vocal apparatus is used in a different way in every language or accent; and a priori in a different way from what you are accustomed to in your own accent when you are learning a new one. There are, perhaps, only a few such basic placements or positions, but they condition the way vowels and consonants sound, and give each accent its own particular resonance and linguistic flavor.

To create an authentic-sounding light native or foreign accent it is sometimes sufficient to have the vocal apparatus positioned as it would be by someone who really speaks with that accent. The accent may then be thickened by adding certain phonetic changes. The general position of the vocal apparatus during speech is determined by four things: the place of articulation of the consonants (see later in this introduction); the positioning of the tongue when forming vowels; how much the lips are protruded; and how tight or loose the muscles are at the corners of the mouth.

Rhythm: Stress Patterns

Rhythm is created by the stress patterns of an accent. Stress indicates which syllables in a word are emphasized or are most prominent. Stressed syllables are usually longer (and louder, and spoken on a pitch differentiating them from adjacent pitches) than the shorter unstressed syllables, just as a half note is longer than a quarter note.

In English every word has its own particular unvarying primary stress, and there is secondary stressing in longer words. However, in British RP and General American, words may be stressed differently. An example is the word *controversy*: in British RP it is pronounced /kuhn TRO vuh see/; in General American, /KAHN truh VOR see/. Unless you have grown up speaking English, and thus learned English stress patterns automatically and unconsciously, you have to make an effort to learn the stress for every word. Stress in English is called "random": words could be stressed on any syllable, and you don't know where the stress is unless you have learned it.

In English, whichever word is stressed is the one that gives a sentence its meaning, not to be understood out of context. Take, for instance, the sentence "I never said he stole my money." Stressing a different word changes the meaning of the sentence; each meaning in parentheses indicates only one of several possibilities:

1. *I* never said he stole my money. (Maybe somebody else said it.)
2. I *never* said he stole my money. (You made that up!)
3. I never *said* he stole my money. (That doesn't mean I didn't think it.)
4. I never said *he* stole my money. (I said somebody else stole it.)
5. I never said he *stole* my money. (I gave it to him.)
6. I never said he stole *my* money. (It belonged to somebody else.)
7. I never said he stole my *money*. (He stole my keys.)

There are languages in which the first syllable of every word is always stressed, and other languages in which stress is always on the last syllable.

Languages in which a particular syllable is always stressed are said to have "uniform" stress. You always know how to stress words correctly even if you have no idea what they mean. This information is very important in creating a foreign accent, as such automatic habits can carry over into English.

The rhythmic stress patterns of a native language are often difficult to break, as they are so ingrained. They tend to carry over into English, although the correct random English stress patterns can be and often are learned. But the French accent, with its tendency to stress the last syllables of phrases, or the Hungarian accent, with its tendency to stress the first syllables of words, show how difficult it is to unlearn habits related to linguistic stress patterns.

Music: Intonation Patterns

Every accent has its own characteristic music, which is made up of a series of pitch or intonation patterns. Intonation means the pattern of pitch changes in connected speech— that is, in a sentence, phrase, or general utterance. All languages communicate by using a combination of pitch and stress, and the pitch and stress patterns are different in different languages. When you learn an accent, you must study these patterns along with the accent's phonetic aspects.

The pitch patterns (intonation patterns) in English express and convey emotion and meaning in ways we have automatically learned. We can choose to emphasize any word by saying it on a different pitch, higher or lower, from the surrounding pitches.

It is very difficult to describe the intonation patterns of any language, but every language has a distinctive intonation pattern, or systematic way of using pitches to express emotion. You simply have to hear them, and to learn what they mean.

Phonetics

You will make the actual sounds of an accent by learning how to do them physically. First, ask yourself how you make the vowel and consonant sounds of your own natural accent. Close your eyes and observe how those sounds "feel" in the mouth, and where they are placed. You can compare them to the new sounds of the accent. If you are an American doing a British RP accent, for instance, the sounds will feel more forward in the mouth than they do in your own accent, and the consonants will be more strongly articulated; that is, whatever muscle or part of the mouth presses against another part—the two lips, for instance, when saying /b/ or /p/—will be stronger in an upper-class British accent than in a General American accent.

Vowels, Semi-Vowels, and Diphthongs

A *vowel* is a single sound made by passing air through the vibrating vocal cords and then through the vocal cavity without the flow of air being stopped. The shape of the vocal cavity changes with each vowel; the tongue is higher or lower, the vocal cavity is more open or more closed, and the lips are relaxed or protruded or retracted, rounded or unrounded. The stream of air is directed up and either primarily to the back or middle or front of the palate (the "sounding board" of the mouth), and this is called the focal point, or what I mean by the point of resonance. Hence we refer, as I have said, to back and front vowels, which can be open or closed, rounded or unrounded. The vowel /ah/ in *father*, for example, is an open back unrounded vowel. There are also, as in French and Portuguese, nasal vowels, pronounced by lowering the soft palate at the back of the mouth and allowing some air to flow through the nasal cavity just above it, as when articulating the consonants /m/ and /n/.

A *semi-vowel* is a vowel during the pronunciation of which the flow of air is beginning to be stopped by the action of tongue or lips. It therefore has almost a consonantal quality. The two semi-vowels in English are /w/, during which the lips are beginning to close and are slightly rounded, and /y/, during which the sides of the tongue move up toward the roof of the mouth touching it very lightly. They can interchangeably be called either semi-consonants or semi-vowels. Both /y/ and /w/ combine with vowels to form diphthongs: /yah/, /ye/, /yee/, /yoh/, /yoo/, /wah/, /we/, /wee/, /woh/, /woo/.

A *diphthong* consists of two vowels, or a vowel and a semi-vowel spoken in one breath. One of the vowels is always stressed. The unstressed half of the diphthong is always very short. An example is /I/, a combination of the /ah/ in *father* and the /ee/ in *meet*; /ah/ is stressed. In the case of diphthongs formed from a semi-vowel and a vowel, the vowel is always stressed: an example is the name of the letter "u" or the word *you*, formed with the semi-vowel /y/ and the vowel /ooh/ as in the word *boot*: /yOOH/. A diphthong occurs when the jaw relaxes slightly immediately after the pronunciation of a vowel and while sound is still issuing from the vocal cords. The tongue "glides" to a different position, changing the shape of the interior of the mouth, and we hear a diphthong.

Consonants

A *consonant* is a sound in which the flow of air is impeded or hindered by the action of tongue, lips, or teeth. Each consonant has a "point, or place, of articulation." The word *articulation* means how parts of the vocal apparatus touch each other to form a sound. For instance, to form a /t/, the tongue touches the palate (the roof of the mouth) just where it starts to curve upward, behind the front teeth—that is its point of articulation. The tongue may apply more or less pressure, and this changes the quality of the sound, making the /t/ hard or soft. In British RP, the /t/ is hard, as it is in the phrase *a cup of tea*. In General American, the /t/ is soft; that is, the pressure made by the tongue is not very strong. Say *a cup of tea* to yourself in both accents, and see how different they "feel" in the mouth.

Every language has its own consonant system, its own "inventory" of consonants. In English there are two versions of certain consonants: "voiced," in which there is sound from the vocal cords, and "voiceless" (or "unvoiced"), in which there is no vibration of the vocal cords. The pairs are, voiced and voiceless respectively: /b/ and /p/; /d/ and /t/; /j/ (/dg/) as in *edge* and /ch/ (/tsh/) as in *church*; /v/ and /f/; /g/ and /k/; /z/ and /s/; /zh/ as in *pleasure* and /sh/ as in *sure*; voiced /th/ as in *there* and voiceless /th/ as in *think*.

A letter is used in spelling to indicate what is actually a range of sounds. For example, the /t/ at the beginning of a word is actually a different sound from the /t/ in the middle of a word, different yet again from the sound at the end of a word: e.g., *tip*, *matter*, *pit*. In the more heavily "aspirated" version of /t/—that is, with breath added to the sound—sometimes heard in the middle of a word like *matter*, the tongue hardly touches the gum ridge and more air is forced through the vocal cavity; this is called a "tapped /t/." The "tapped /d/," heard as a substitute for voiced /th/ in some native and foreign accents in words like *other* and in some native accents in words like *whatever*, is also very important in accent work.

For all accents, native and foreign, always look at the consonants /l/, /r/, and /th / th/. These consonants are called "continuants," because their sounds can be continued as long as the speaker has breath. The /r/ sounds are especially important in any accent:

1. **Rhotic sounds:** Rhotic sounds are the voiced consonants spelled with the letter "r." (The word *rhotic* comes from the name of a Greek letter of the alphabet, *rho*.) The sound associated with this letter in another language is often carried into English in a foreign accent. Is "r" after a vowel—"post-vocalic"—pronounced, or is it as silent as the "b" in *lamb*? When post-vocalic letter "r" is pronounced, the accent is "rhotic"—as in a General American or Scottish accent. When post-vocalic "r" is not pronounced, the accent is "non-rhotic"—as in

a British RP accent. One of the first questions to ask when studying any accent is whether it is rhotic or non-rhotic.

2. **Native accents:** In English, /r/ is a "retroflex" consonant; that is, the tip of the tongue curls upward so that the bottom of the tongue is toward the palate when the sound is articulated. The hardness or softness of the sound depends on whether or not the back of the tongue is relaxed. For instance, in U.S. Midwestern accents it is slightly tensed, and in British RP it is relaxed. In accents native to English, if /r/ is not pronounced it still often influences the vowel which precedes it, because the tongue is beginning to curl upward as if to articulate an /r/, thus giving an impression of the letter /r/. Therefore, we speak of "r-influenced" vowels. In upper-class British English, post-vocalic /r/ is silent, with some exceptions. In General American, post-vocalic /r/ is pronounced, but it is silent in certain regional accents of the U.S. such as New York or some areas of the East Coast of the South. In some accents, among them British RP, Scottish, or certain Irish accents, a lightly trilled or tapped /r/ is sometimes heard.

3. **Foreign accents:** Is the /r/ in a foreign language trilled frontally, as in Italian or Spanish? Is /r/ pronounced from the back of the throat (a "uvular /r/"), as in French or German? Is /r/ pronounced in the middle of the mouth, with the tip of the tongue curving upward slightly so that the bottom of the tongue is toward the palate, as it is in General American or Mandarin?

4. **The trilled /r/:** To pronounce a trilled /r/ (with one or more taps or flaps) heard in many other languages, including Spanish, Italian, Swedish, Finnish, Basque, Portuguese, Polish, Russian and Czech, begin by saying a tapped /d/: the tongue makes a minimal, quick pressure when the /d/ is articulated, as in the famous phrase, *FuggeDabouDit*. Then say the word *very* with a /d/ instead of an /r/. Draw the tip of the tongue back a very little bit and drop your tongue slightly until you have the impression of saying /r/. Do not curl the bottom of your tongue toward the roof of the mouth. The tip of the tongue

should be just at the opening of the palate in back of the gum ridge. Alternatively, you may begin a trilled /r/ by saying *hurrah* and shortening the vowel in the first syllable until it is entirely eliminated, leaving you with a very breathy sound: /hr/. Continue tapping the tip of the tongue lightly against the opening of the palate, hardly touching it at all. You can then eliminate the /h/.

5. **The uvular /r/:** To pronounce the uvular or guttural voiced /r/ heard in various versions in French, German, Yiddish, Dutch, Danish, Norwegian, and Hebrew, first lower the tip of the tongue so it touches the back of the lower front teeth, then raise the back of the tongue so the uvula vibrates against it, as in gargling, or as in articulating its voiceless version, the /kh/ sound heard in Scottish *loch* or German *Ach!* This consonant is, in fact, the voiceless one in the pair /kh/ and uvular /r/, which is a voiced consonant.

Some Questions to Ask Yourself

Select the accent to suit the character and make it your own by constant repetition and drilling. Whether you do a real or comically distorted accent, it must be organic and, therefore, internal to the character.

1. Is the accent rhotic or non-rhotic? In a foreign accent, does the native /r/ carry over into the accent in English?
2. How is /l/ pronounced—with the back of the tongue raised, as in Russian, or with the tip of the tongue well forward, as in French?
3. How are /th / *th*/ sounds pronounced—correctly, or are substitute sounds such as /d/ and /t/ used?
4. How do the vowels and diphthongs differ from your own accent?
5. What is the character's social and educational background? For instance, there are U.K. accents native to English associated with social classes.

6. If a character is from a foreign linguistic background, how did he or she learn English? A professor of physics who learned English at his European, African, or Asian university may speak with a more upper-class accent in English than a laborer who learned English on the streets of an English or American city. Did the character learn English at school, or on the streets of New York or London or Sydney or Johannesburg?

7. How well and how grammatically does the character speak the English language, as indicated in the script? This will often tell you how heavy the accent should be, whether it is native or foreign.

8. How thick or heavy or light is the accent? We sometimes hear such a slight accent that we cannot quite identify it. As an actor you may wish to create such an accent, or you may want to do an accent that is just a bit more identifiable to an audience. People can also be inconsistent within their own accent, and will sometimes pronounce /r/ or /th/ correctly, and sometimes not. As an actor, you should make sure that any accent you do is clearly understood, however thick the original may be in real life.

9. At what age did the person learn English? Below the age of twelve a heavy foreign accent is very rare, if indeed any exists at all. I know people who learned English as a second language, and grew up in New York City. They sound like New Yorkers speaking General American, and have not even a trace of the accent associated with their first language, which they also continue to speak. But even such brilliant people as Einstein and Freud, both of whom learned English comparatively late in life, spoke with very thick German and Viennese accents, respectively. Einstein even had to be subtitled in newsreels.

10. Where can I find actual examples of the accent, used by real people? You want to listen to and if possible record these examples. Embassies, consulates, movies, and restaurants with personnel who come from the country provide some excellent source material. Listening to a good dialect coach is all very well, but you want to

find actual examples and do the work yourself of analyzing what you are hearing.

An Exercise for Teaching Yourself Any Accent

You can use this exercise for studying the practice exercises and monologues at the end of each chapter.

When you know what the sounds of the accent are, and how they "shift" from the sounds you usually make, go through a script you are working on, a book you are reading, or any material you like, and select one sound. You might select /th / *th*/ substitutes, for instance, or a diphthong shift to a pure vowel, such as /oh/ to /aw/. Mark the sounds in some way, then go through the material again, speaking aloud and pronouncing only those sounds.

Do this for all the sound shifts, adding one each time. Do each new sound together with the ones you did previously. Eventually, you will have all the required sounds in place. Also, as you do this, be aware of exactly what the muscles of the mouth are doing, and you will concentrate on the correct positioning or placement of the lips, tongue, and the opening of the mouth, wider or more closed as required.

You will thus become aware of how the whole accent that you have gradually built up feels in the mouth, and you can then make all of that into a habit.

When you have finished this part of the exercise, continue by writing out your own pronunciation using the list of phonetic symbols in this book, or the International Phonetic Alphabet (IPA), if you are familiar with it. Record yourself and listen carefully until you are satisfied that you have achieved the desired sound.

You will then be able to pick up any material and read it with the accent. Once you can do this, you have mastered the accent and it is now part of your actor's toolkit.

1
The General American Accent

The United States of America has no official language, but the vast majority of the population of all ethnic backgrounds speaks Standard American English (StAmE), taught in schools nationwide, and used in government, the professions, and the media. Most people speak StAmE in a colloquial manner that differs from the formal style employed in writing, and in spoken presentations of all kinds.

Teach Yourself the General American Accent

There is no standard accent in the United States, with its many Northern and Southern regional and urban speech patterns, but there is a ubiquitous non-regional accent called General American. With slight variations, such as General Californian English, it is the most widely used pronunciation of StAmE.

Actors used to be taught a cultivated "stage" accent—an older version of General American—exemplified in the beautifully articulated speech of many Hollywood movie actors of the 1930s and 1940s, no matter where they came from, including Greer Garson, from London, England; George Brent, from Dublin, Ireland; William Powell, from Pittsburgh, Pennsylvania; and Myrna Loy, from Helena, Montana. Edith Skinner, in her magisterial textbook *Speak with Distinction* (Applause, 1990), first published in

1942, called this accent American Theatre Standard; it is also called Mid-Atlantic or Transatlantic speech. Her book remains a classic, and provides excellent exercises for clear enunciation and perfect diction, even though the accent itself has been largely gone since the late 1960s.

1. **Positioning, placement, and use of the muscles of the mouth during speech:** The general position of the mouth muscles, including the corners of the lips, is relaxed. The accent "feels" as though it is pronounced in the middle of the mouth.

2. **The sound of /r/:** Post-vocalic (after a vowel) /r/, spelled with the letter "r," is lightly pronounced. This /r/ is always retroflex, with the bottom of the tongue curled slightly up toward the palate. The back of the tongue is relaxed.

3. **Vowels, semi-vowels, and diphthongs:** The vowels of Standard American English are /a/, /ah/, /aw/, /e/, /uh/ (the schwa), /ih/, /ee/, /o/, /o/, /oo/, /ooh/, and /u/. The semi-vowels are /w/ and /y/. See the list of phonetic symbols for their pronunciations and for a complete list of diphthongs.

   The vowels are spelled "a," "e," "i," "o," and "u," but there is no single sound attached to any of these letters in English orthography: for example, /u/ may be spelled with a "u" in *but* or with an "o" in *love*.

   a. **The sound of /a/:** This vowel in *cat* and *that* is pronounced with the mouth open in a medium position, neither too wide nor too closed. It is used in the "ask list," presented later in this chapter.

   b. **The sound of /aw/:** The pure vowel /aw/ in such words as *law, talk,* and *walk* is long, and pronounced with the lips slightly protruded.

   c. **The sound of /o/:** In such words as *got, hot,* and *not, /ah/* is used, rather than the short /o/ of British RP or Canadian English, although /o/ is heard as well, particularly in the speech of older Americans.

   d. **The sound of /oh/:** This diphthong is composed of the short /o/ in *hot* (not the /u/ in *but* heard in some regional accents), the stressed half of the diphthong; and the /ooh/ in *boot: home* /HOoohM/.

e. **Three distinct vowels:** The /a/ in *marry* /MA ree/, the /e/ in *merry* /ME ree/, and the intermediate open vowel where the mouth is open wider than for /e/ and diphthongized in *Mary* /MEuh ree/ are each differentiated. But in certain regional accents, especially in the Midwest and parts of the South, all three words rhyme and are pronounced like *Mary*: *marry* /MEuh ree/, *merry* /MEuh ree/, *Mary* /MEuh ree/.

f. **Vowels in unstressed syllables; the schwa /uh/:** Vowels in many unstressed syllables are often given a full value: *bereft* /bee (alternatively, buh) REFT/, *February* /FE brooh E ree/, *territory* /TE rih TAW ree/—and not /TE rih tree/, as in British RP. A schwa—the sound of "e" in *the* before a consonant: *the story* /thuh STAW ree/—often replaces an unstressed vowel: *committee* /kuh MIH tee/, *garrulous* /GA ruh luhs/, *history* /HIH stuh ree/, *suddenly* /SU duhn (alternatively, dn) lee/.

4. **Other consonants:** Consonants are well articulated, and not too hard; that is, the pressure of one articulator on another—for instance, the pressure of the tongue against the palate at the gum ridge near the upper front teeth (the upper alveolar ridge) to form a /t/ or a /d/—is not usually very strong. See the introduction for a discussion of voiced and voiceless consonants; and consult the list of symbols for a complete listing.

a. **The sounds of /l/:** In a General American initial /l/, as in the word *like*, the tongue is relaxed; its tip touches the upper alveolar ridge lightly, while its sides and blade are raised, without much pressure on the palate.

b. **Tapped /d/:** Instead of a fully articulated /t/ between words, a tapped /d/, sometimes called a flapped /d/, is usual. The tapped /d/ is articulated by touching the tongue to the place where /d/ is articulated. The tip of the tongue comes quickly away from the back of the upper gum ridge without making the pressure that would form a fully realized /d/: *at all* /a DAWL/, *it isn't true* /ih

DIH zuhnt trooh/. Note that the final /t/ in *isn't* in this phrase is usually dropped, since the word *true* begins with a /t/; in other words, the first /t/ is "assimilated" into the second /t/.

c. **Tapped and aspirated /t/:** The voiceless tapped /t/ is articulated in the same way as a tapped /d/. The heavily aspirated (with the tongue not touching the gum ridge, but allowing air between them) tapped /t/ is sometimes heard in such words as *matter*: /MA tuhr/, *pity* /PIH tee/, *what a pity* /WAH duh PIH tee (alternatively, dee)/ or /WAH tuh uh PIH tee/, with both /t/ sounds tapped. But a fully realized /t/ is also often heard in those words.

d. **The sounds of /th / th/:** These voiced and voiceless consonants, respectively, are correctly pronounced all the time. To pronounce these consonants, simultaneously place the tip of your tongue loosely behind the upper front teeth, to allow air to get through the opening; tense the tongue's raised sides, which are held against the rows of teeth on both sides; and raise and tense the back of the tongue slightly.

e. **Consonant clusters:** All consonants in consonant clusters are pronounced: *expect* /ek SPEKT/, *hold fast* /HOHLD FAST/, *ghosts* /GOHSTS/, *into the depths* /IHN tooh thuh DEP*TH*S/, *he reacts to ghosts tremblingly* /hee ree AKTS tooh GOHSTS TREM blihng lee/, *red leather* /RED LE thuhr/.

The Ask List

This is a partial list of words that are pronounced in General American and in most regional and urban accents by all social classes with the /a/ in *that* in stressed syllables, as opposed to the British RP pronunciation of these words with the open-throated vowel /ah/. The old-fashioned Down East Maine and Boston accents are exceptions for a few of these words, but the /ah/ in these accents and in General American is not as open-throated and does not resonate as far back as the British version of the vowel.

advantage, after (and words beginning and ending with "after": *after-noon, afterwards, hereafter,* etc.), *answer, ask, aunt* (sometimes heard as /AHNT/, or /AWNT/), *banana, basket, bastard, bath, blast, branch, brass, broadcast, calf, can't, cask, casket, cast, caste, castle, chance, chancellor, chant, clasp, class* (and words beginning with "class": *classmate, class-room, classy,* etc.), *command, countermand, daft, dance, demand, disaster, downcast, draft, enchant, entrance* (verb), *example, fast, fasten, gala, ghastly, glance, glass, graft, grant,* words ending in "-graph": *paragraph, photograph, telegraph,* etc., words ending in "-graphical": *geographical, topographical,* etc., *grasp, grass, half, lance, last, lather, laugh, mask, mast, master, nasty, outcast, pass, passing, past, pastor, pastoral, path, perchance, plant, plaster, prance, raft, rascal, rasp, raspberry, rather, reprimand, salve, sample, shaft, shan't, slander, slant, staff, stanch, task, trance, transcript, transport* (and other words beginning with the prefix "trans-"), *vast, wrath*

Intonation and Stress: The Music and Rhythm of the Accent

There are four or five pitches in a typical sentence in General American accents.

Stressed and important syllables—whatever syllables the speaker wishes to emphasize—are usually spoken on an upper pitch, with more muscular force than is used for unstressed syllables, and they are louder. Unstressed and unimportant syllables are spoken on a lower pitch. This pitch pattern (intonation) creates the typical rise and fall of a sentence. In emphasizing a particular syllable, the speaker may use a lower, rather than a higher, pitch.

Stressed syllables may also be spoken on more than one pitch, with a rising or falling tone. Because of the prevalence of diphthongs in English, it is easy to use these tones: one half of the diphthong is at one end of the rise or fall, and the other half is at the other end.

The end of a simple declarative sentence is spoken on a lower pitch.

At the end of a question the pitch rises, but this pattern may change. For example, if the word *are* is stressed in *How are you?*, it may be spoken on an upper pitch, and *you* on a lower one.

An imperative, or a command, is usually spoken with a falling tone at the end.

Emotional utterances, such as expletives, may add several pitches to the pattern. Anger is expressed with raised pitches and at a louder volume, but also—and this can be very effective for actors—in low, even tones, with the anger seething underneath.

Practice Exercises

1. *Trying to argue with someone who has renounced the use of reason is like administering medicine to the dead. —Thomas Paine*
/TRI ihng tooh AHR gyooh with SUM wun hooh haz ree NOWNTSD thuh YOOHS uhv REE zuhn ihz lIk ad MIH nuh stuh rihng MED ih suhn tuh (alternatively, tooh) thuh DED/ /TAHM uhs PAYN/

2. *Suppose you were an idiot and suppose you were a member of Congress; but I repeat myself. —Samuel Langhorne Clemens, known as Mark Twain*
/suh POHZ yooh wor an IH dee uht and suh POHZ yooh wor uh MEM buhr uhv KAHN gruhs buh DI ree PEET mI SELF/ /SA myooh uhl LANG HAWRN KLE muhnz / NOHN az (alternatively, uhz) MAHRK TWAYN/

Notes: The /d/ in the pronunciation syllable /DI/ is tapped. The /r/ sounds at the end of *were* and *member* may be linked to *an* and *of*: /wo ran/, /MEM buh ruhv/; if you link these /r/ sounds, keep the /r/ light.

3.   *Once upon a midnight dreary, while I pondered weak and weary,*
       Over many a quaint and curious volume of forgotten lore,
       While I nodded, nearly napping, suddenly there came a tapping,
       As of someone gently rapping, rapping at my chamber door.

"'Tis some visitor," I muttered, "tapping at my chamber door—
Only this, and nothing more."
—From "The Raven" by Edgar Allan Poe

/WUNTS uh PAHN uh MIHD NIT DRIHuh ree wIl I PAHN duhrd WEEK
and WIHuh ree

OH vuhr ME nee uh KWAYNT and KYOOH ree uhs VAHL yoohm uhv for
GAH tuhn LAWR

wIl I NAH dihd NIHuhr lee NA pihng SU duhn lee theuhr KAYM uh TA
pihng

az uhv SUM wun JENT lee RA pihng RA pihng at mI CHAYM buhr DAWR

tihz sum VIH zih tuhr I MU tuhrd TA pihng at mI CHAYM buhr DAWR

OHN lee THIHS and NU thihng MAWR/

/FRUM thuh RAY vuhn bI ED guhr A luhn POH/

4. From Louisa May Alcott's *Little Men: Life at Plumfield with Jo's Boys*
(1871), chapter 1: "Nat"

"Please, sir, is this Plumfield?" asked a ragged boy of the man who
opened the great gate at which the omnibus left him.

"Yes. Who sent you?"

"Mr. Laurence. I have got a letter for the lady."

"All right; go up to the house, and give it to her; she'll see to
you, little chap."

The man spoke pleasantly, and the boy went on, feeling much
cheered by the words. Through the soft spring rain that fell on
sprouting grass and budding trees, Nat saw a large square house
before him—a hospitable-looking house, with an old-fashioned
porch, wide steps, and lights shining in many windows. Neither
curtains nor shutters hid the cheerful glimmer; and, pausing a
moment before he rang, Nat saw many little shadows dancing on
the walls, heard the pleasant hum of young voices, and felt that it

was hardly possible that the light and warmth and comfort within could be for a homeless "little chap" like him.

Monologues

1. From Eugene O'Neill's *Long Day's Journey Into Night* (1956), Act 4

This autobiographical, posthumously produced play is the story of an aspiring writer, Edmund, a sensitive youth suffering from tuberculosis; his morphine-addicted mother, Mary; his ne'er-do-well, unstable older brother, Jamie; and his miserly father, James Tyrone, once a famous actor who has now taken to drink. Late at night, Tyrone and Edmund have a heart-to-heart talk.

In Sidney Lumet's 1962 film version, Ralph Richardson plays Tyrone; Katharine Hepburn is Mary; Jason Robards reprises his Broadway role as Jamie; and Dean Stockwell is an effective, moving Edmund.

EDMUND: You've just told me some high spots in your memories. Want to hear mine? They're all connected with the sea. Here's one. When I was on the Squarehead square rigger, bound for Buenos Aires. Full moon in the Trades. The old hooker driving fourteen knots. I lay on the bowsprit, facing astern, with the water foaming into spume under me, the masts with every sail white in the moonlight, towering high above me. I became drunk with the beauty and singing rhythm of it, and for a moment I lost myself— actually lost my life. I was set free! I dissolved in the sea, became white sails and flying spray, became beauty and rhythm, became moonlight and the ship and the high dim-starred sky!

2. From Tina Howe's *The Art of Dining* (1978), Act 2, Scene 2

Set in The Golden Carrousel, an elegant gourmet restaurant on the New Jersey shore, this comedy centers on Elizabeth Barrow Colt, a painfully shy and awkward short-story writer "in her early thirties." In the following scene, she is dining with her publisher.

ELIZABETH BARROW COLT: We ate every night at 8 o'clock sharp because my parents didn't start their cocktail hour until 7, but since dinnertime was meant for exchanging news of the day, the emphasis was always on talking . . . and not on eating. My father bolted his food, and my mother played with hers: sculpting it up into hills and then mashing it back down with her fork. To make things worse, before we sat down at the table she'd always put on a fresh smear of lipstick. I still remember the shade. It was called "Fire and Ice . . ." a dark throbbing red that rubbed off on her fork in waxy clumps that stained her food pink, so that by the end of the first course she'd have rended everything into a kind of . . . rosy puree. As my father wolfed down his meat and vegetables, I'd watch my mother thread this puree through the raised acorns on her plate, fanning it out into long runny pink ribbons . . . I could never eat a thing.

3. From Emily Mann's *Still Life* (1981), Act 2, Scene 4, "The Spaghetti Story"

Vietnam War veteran Mark is married to Cheryl, whom he abuses, and is having an affair with Nadine. The play's title comes from the fact that, after Mark beats up Cheryl, he always buys her a work of art.

CHERYL: Every day before Thanksgiving Mark does a spaghetti dinner, and this is a traditional thing. [. . .] He makes ravioli, lasagne, spaghetti, meatballs, three different kinds of spaghetti sauces: shrimp, plain, meat sauce. Oh, he makes gnocci [*sic*]! He makes his own noodles! And it's good. He's a damn good cook for Italian food. But you can imagine what I go through for three weeks for that party to feed forty people. Sit-down dinner. He insists it's a sit-down dinner. [. . .] We heated the porch last year because we did not have enough room to seat forty people. And I run around serving all these slobs, and this is the first year he's really charged anyone. And we lose on it every year. I mean, we lose, first year we lost $300. This dinner is a $500 deal. I'm having a baby this November, and if he thinks he's having any kind of spaghetti dinner, he can get his butt out of here. I can't take it.

4. From Larry Kramer's *The Normal Heart* (1985), Act 2, Scene 11

The first play to deal with the horror of the AIDS epidemic, this acclaimed drama was instrumental in publicizing the growing tragedy that had beset not only America and the LGBT community, but also the world.

Ned Weeks is a gay, temperamental, Jewish-American man who has founded an advocacy group for AIDS victims in New York City. Ned's friend Bruce Niles has recently been to see Dr. Emma Brookner, a doctor involved in treating patients with the mysterious illness. Bruce explains to Ned what happened to their friend Albert. Ned hadn't known he was ill.

BRUCE: No one did. He wouldn't tell anyone. Do you know why? Because of me. Because he knows I'm so scared I'm some sort of carrier. This makes three people I've been with who are dead. I went to Emma and I begged her: please test me somehow, please tell me if I'm giving this to people. And she said she couldn't, there isn't any way they can find out anything because they still don't know what they're looking for. Albert, I think I loved him best of all, and he went so fast. His mother wanted him back in Phoenix before he died, this was last week when it was obvious, so I get permission from Emma and bundle him all up and take him to the plane in an ambulance. The pilot wouldn't take off and I refused to leave the plane—you would have been proud of me—so finally they get another pilot. Then, after we take off, Albert loses his mind, not recognizing me, not knowing where he is or that he's going home, and then, right there, on the plane, he becomes . . . incontinent.

2
Northern U.S. Regional Accents: The Midwest

General American is the usual accent in the areas listed here, as well as in California and Alaska. It coexists with regional variations in the Midwestern, Western, and Pacific Northwestern states—Colorado, Idaho, Illinois, Indiana, Iowa, Kansas (the south of which features some areas with Southern-sounding accents), Michigan, Minnesota, Montana, Nebraska, North and South Dakota, Ohio, Oregon, Utah, Washington, Wisconsin, and Wyoming. This is also the case for the Middle Atlantic states of the Eastern seaboard—Delaware, coastal Maryland, New Jersey, New York, Pennsylvania; and those of New England—Connecticut, Maine, Massachusetts, New Hampshire, Rhode Island, and Vermont.

Although Northern regional accents are generally rhotic—post-vocalic (after a vowel) /r/ is pronounced lightly or heavily, depending on the area—there are pockets of non-rhotic accents in which post-vocalic /r/ is not pronounced, especially on the Northern East Coast. East Coast accents change as you head north, so that coastal Maryland, including Baltimore, sounds quite different from coastal Maine. Down East Maine, also called Down Home Maine, is largely a coastal accent, but heard inland as well. This old-fashioned pronunciation is non-rhotic, with a silent post-vocalic /r/. It is perfect for some of the plays of Eugene O'Neill—especially the "sea plays" and *Desire Under the Elms* (1924). It is perhaps best to ignore the phonetics as he writes them, though they do inform you that the characters have this accent. Down East Maine's most famous, frequently heard expression is *Ayeh* /AY uh/, for yes. The accent shares some of the same vowel shifts as the Boston accent, namely the /a/ to /ah/ shift in such words as *can't* and *bath*. Vowels are quite short in general. The /aw/ sound before /r/ in words such as *door, for, folklore, important, last*, and *or* is pronounced /ah/: /DAH/, /FAH/, /FOHK lah/, /ihm PAH tnt/, /LAHST/, /AH/. Sometimes, alternatively, a schwa is inserted in such words as *floor* and *door*: /FLOHuh/, /DOHuh/. The final /g/ in "-ing" verb endings is often dropped. See *Dolores Claiborne* (1995) for examples of typical Maine accents, which Kathy Bates (from Memphis, Tennessee), Christopher Plummer (from Toronto, Canada), and the rest of the cast do perfectly.

Coastal Maryland, including the city of Baltimore, has rhotic accents, with post-vocalic (after a vowel) /r/ pronounced. Philadelphia, Pennsylvania, and Baltimore share characteristic pronunciations of /oh/ (also heard in southern New Jersey), /Eooh/ and /Oooh/, as opposed to the General American /Oooh/: *I know* /I NEooh/. In Baltimore, consonants are regularly dropped in the middle of words, so, for instance, *everybody* is pronounced /E ruh (alternatively, ER, or E ree) BAH dee/, with a tapped /d/, a pronunciation also heard in accents all over the South. Typical Baltimore pronunciations include *everything* /E ree THIHNG/, *haunted* /HAW nihd/, *Saturday* /SAR dee/, and *totally* /TOH lee/; *Saturday everything was totally booked* /SAR dee E ree THIHNG wuz TOH lee BOOKT/. Natives pronounce the name of their city /BAHL duh (alternatively, uh) MOOHR/, with a tapped /d/; it is /BAWL tuh MAWR/ in General American.

In this chapter, we will concentrate on the accents of the Midwest, with special practice exercises for Michigan as an example. For a Michigan accent, listen to Michael Moore in his many documentaries, and on DVDs of his television series *The Awful Truth* (1999–2000). And for another Midwestern accent, see chapter 7 on Chicago.

For strong Midwestern accents, listen to the actors in *Fargo* (1996), set in Minnesota. The clear Nebraska accent of Johnny Carson, which can be heard on videos of the old *Tonight Show* (1962–1992), and the clean Indiana accent of David Letterman on his show (*Late Show with David Letterman*,

1993–) are very close to General American. For typical, light Midwestern accents with excellent diction, listen to Clark Gable from Ohio; Spencer Tracy from Milwaukee, Wisconsin; Gary Cooper from Montana; and James Stewart, born in the town of Indiana, in western Pennsylvania.

Teach Yourself Midwestern U.S. Accents

1. **Positioning, placement, and use of the muscles of the mouth during speech:** The general position of the muscles during speech in the Midwestern accents feels very tight and the lips are drawn out to the sides a bit, as in a tight smile, depending on the area. The accents "feel" as though they are pronounced in the middle of the mouth. The back of the tongue is tensed slightly during speech.

2. **The sounds of /r/:** These are strongly rhotic accents generally, with a very hard retroflex /r/, at the ends of words and before another consonant. The tip of the tongue rolled back and up, more than it is in General American; and the back of the tongue is automatically tensed. This is true of Upstate New York, western Pennsylvania, Idaho, Indiana, Illinois, Ohio, Montana, Wisconsin, Minnesota, Michigan, Nebraska, and the Dakotas. For the East Coast and the Pacific Northwest (Washington, Oregon, Idaho), make the /r/ softer.

   a. **/r/ insertion:** In western Pennsylvania, Indiana, and elsewhere farther west, an /r/ is sometimes inserted after /aw/, so *wash* (General American pronunciation: /WAHSH/) is pronounced /WAWRSH/. This is also true of certain areas of New England, such as parts of Rhode Island, where the accent is strongly non-rhotic.

3. **Vowels and diphthongs:**

   a. **The sound of /a/:** This vowel in *cat* and *that* is very flat, and sometimes diphthongized to /Auh/, especially in Michigan and northern Wisconsin. The back of the tongue is automatically tensed and the mouth slightly more closed than in General American for this open vowel.

b. **The shifts from /aw/ to /ah/ and from /ah/ to /aw/:** Shift the long /aw/ of General American in such words as *law*, *talk*, and *walk* to the short /ah/ for the entire Midwest and Pacific Northwest. The vowel /ah/ is pronounced with the lips not protruded but open wide. In some words, such as *wash*, the General American /ah/ shifts to a long /aw/.

c. **The shift from /ay/ to /ee/:** The diphthong /ay/ sometimes shifts to /ee/, especially when it is unstressed (the Dakotas, Minnesota, Wisconsin).

d. **The schwa:** The schwa is used in words like *there*, when unstressed, and *sure* /SHUHR/: *There sure is* /thuhr SHUHR ihz/. This is also the case in Detroit, Minneapolis, upstate Wisconsin, and in Minnesota on the Canadian border, where the vowel is shorter than it is in Detroit. A typical Wisconsin and Minnesota phrase, often parodied, and heard in *Fargo*, is *Oh, sure, you betcha* /oh SHUHR yooh BE chuh/.

e. **The shift from /e/ to /ay/:** An important shift, heard in many parts of the Midwest from western Pennsylvania, Indiana, and Missouri (with its Southern accent), and in parts of California as well, is from General American /e/ to /ay/, in such words as *measure*, *leisure*, and *pleasure*, pronounced /MAY zhuhr/, /LAY (alternatively, LEE) zhuhr/, /PLAY zhuhr/.

f. **The shift from /oh/ to /ooh/:** Typical of Michigan, northern Wisconsin, and Minnesota accents is the closing of the diphthong /oh/, which shifts to /ooh/. *I know* is pronounced /I nooh/.

g. **The shift from /ooh/ to /oo/:** In such words as *roof* and *room*, where General American pronunciation has the vowel /ooh/, Midwestern accents often have /oo/: /ROOF/, /ROOM/, as opposed to General American /ROOHF/, /ROOHM/.

h. **The shift from /oy/ to /I/:** This shift is typical of northern Wisconsin. The infamous Senator Joseph McCarthy's phrase *Point of* *order, Mr. Chairman* is pronounced /PINT uhv AHR duhr MIHS tuhr CHER muhn/.

i. **Three distinct vowels eliminated:** In General American, the /a/ in *marry*, the /e/ in *merry*, and the intermediate, diphthongized open vowel /Euh/ in *Mary* /MEuh ree/ are each differentiated. But in the Midwest and Pacific Northwest accents, all three words rhyme and are pronounced like *Mary*.

4. **Other consonants:** Consonants are hard and well articulated. Final /d/, /k/, /p/, /t/, and /z/ are very hard, as they are in Detroit, for instance.

Intonation and Stress: The Music and Rhythm of the Accents

The stress patterns are the same as in General American. The intonation is often very "flat," without much music.

Practice Exercises

1. *Do they know how far we gotta go? Sure they do.*
Wisconsin: /duh thay nooh how FAHR wee GAH duh GOH / SHUHR thee dooh/

Note: The /d/ in the syllable /duh/ is tapped. See p. 17 for the articulation of the tapped /d/.

2. *I'd like to comment about that. I want to say a word about our political process.*
General Midwest, Seattle: /Id LIK tuh KAH ment uh BOWT that / I WAW nuh SAY uh WORD uh BOWT AHR PLIH dih kl PRAH ses/

Notes: The /d/ sounds in the syllables /dih/ and /dI/ are tapped. In Minnesota, the word *political* might be pronounced /puh LIH dee kuhl/, with the /d/ tapped. In Michigan, the word *comment* is pronounced /KA ment/.

3. *I thought they ought to pay cash on the barrelhead just for good measure.*
Indiana, Western Pennsylvania: /I *THA*HT thay AH duh PAY KAYSH awn thuh BE ruhl HAYD just (alternatively, jihst) fuhr good MAY zhuhr/

Notes: The /d/ in the syllable /duh/ is tapped. The /e/ in the syllable /BE/ is long.

4. *Can you turn that off, or at least turn it down? It's awfully loud.*
/kihn (alternatively, KAuhn) yooh TORN THEuh DAHF uhr uht (alternatively, auht) LEEST TORN iht down / ihts AHF lee LOWD/

Notes: The /d/ in the syllable /DAHF/ is tapped. In Michigan and Minnesota, the final consonants, such as /d/ in *loud*, /n/ in *can*, and /t/ in *least*, would be very hard; also, the diphthong /ow/ in *loud* and *down* is pronounced /AHooh/ and is very short. In Michigan, the /a/ in *that* is particularly flat, and the /r/ is very hard. In Indiana, the consonants are softer.

Michigan Practice Exercises
1. *I know that's true and I send my acknowledgments to Congress.*
/I NOOH THAuhTS TROOH Auhnd I SEND mI ak NA luhj muhnts tuh KAN gruhs/

Notes: All the /o/ sounds in such words as *hot* and *not* shift to the /a/ in *that*: /HAT/, /NAT/. Further examples: The prefix "non-" is pronounced /NAN/; the word *comment* is said as /KA ment/; and the word *acknowledgments* sounds like /ak NA luhj muhnts/; *Congress* is pronounced /KAN gruhs/. The retroflex /r/ in Michigan is very hard, with the back of the tongue tensed.

2. *Detroit is a wonderful city and a great place to live.*
Detroit: /DEE troyt ihz uh WUN duhr fool SIH dee Auhn uh GREET PLAYS tuh LIHV/

Note: People from Detroit often stress the first syllable of the city's name; most of Northern America stresses the last syllable, while the first syllable is often stressed in the South.

3. *He's the most impossible person. If you have orange juice he wants pear juice, and vice versa. It's such a bother!*
Detroit: /heez thuh MOHST ihm PAS uh buhl POR suhn / ihf yooh HEuhV AWRNJ JOOHS hee WAHNTS PEuhR joohs Auhnd VIS VOR sah / ihts SUCH uh BA thuhr/

4. *Oh, my God, were you at the Old Cider Mill at the same time? I didn't see you there!*
Detroit: /oh mI GAD wor yooh Auht thee OOHLD SAY duhr MIHL Auht thuh SEEM TIM / I DIHD nt SEE yooh THEuhR/

Note: The /d/ in the syllable /duhr/ is tapped.

Monologues

1. From Tennessee Williams's *Small Craft Warnings* (1972), Act 1

This drama is set in Monk's Place, a "bar along the Southern California Coast." Bobby, one of the castoffs and drifters who frequent the place, is from Iowa.

> BOBBY: In Goldenfield, Iowa, there was a man like that, ran a flower shop with a back room, decorated Chinese, with incense and naked pictures, which he invited boys into. I heard about it. Well, things like that aren't tolerated for long in towns like Goldenfield. There's suspicion and talk and then public outrage and action, and he had to leave so quick he didn't clear out the shop. (*The bar lights have faded and the special spot illuminates* BOBBY.) A bunch of us entered one night. The drying-up flowers rattled in the wind and the wind-chimes tinkled and the . . .

naked pictures were just . . . pathetic, y'know. Except for a sketch of Michelangelo's *David*. I don't think anyone noticed me snatch it off the wall and stuff it into my pocket. Dreams . . . images . . . nights . . . On the plains of Nebraska I passed a night with a group of runaway kids my age and it got cold after sunset. A lovely wild young girl invited me under a blanket with just a smile, and then a boy, me between, and both of them kept saying "love," one of 'em in one ear and one in the other, till I didn't know which was which "love" in which ear or which . . . touch . . . The plain was high and the night air . . . exhilarating and the touches not heavy.

2. From Matt Williams's *Between Daylight and Boonville* (1980), Act 1
Marlene is a miner's wife, a "large-boned woman of about thirty-five years old, though she looks somewhat older." She is seven months pregnant. Marlene and her family live in a temporary trailer court in the southern Indiana mining country. She is talking with two of her friends, Lorette and Carla, also miners' wives, in the trailer park's "recreation area" about a fight she had with her husband.

MARLENE: This one time, before the kids were born, Big Jim was workin' construction before goin' to work for the company. And we were rentin' a little furnished house. I worked all day gettin' the house cleaned up. Baked cookies. Did the wash. It was one of those days. I use to do a lot more of that stuff than I do now. Anyway, I was beat. So, I sit down on the couch and propped my feet on the coffee table and started readin' my magazines. Well, Big Jim comes home from work mad as hell at this young, cocky foreman he's workin' for. So he takes it out on me. He had stopped and had a few beers and picked up a six-pack on his way home. And he walks in and wants to know why I've got my feet propped up on the good coffee table. I told him not to worry about it. It was rented. And he said, "Don't talk back. Take your feet down off the table." I said no. And he said you better. And I said you take them down for me. And he said, "Like hell!" And he yanked that table out from under my feet, went to the front door and threw the coffee table right out into the middle of the front yard. I didn't say a word. I got up, grabbed his six-pack and walked over and threw it right out in the front yard.

3. Two Monologues from Kathleen Tolan's *A Weekend Near Madison* (1983)

Weekend guests in the home of psychiatrist David and his wife, Doe, near Madison, Wisconsin, include the lesbian singer Nessa, her lover Samantha, and David's younger brother, Jim, who had been Nessa's lover before she came out. Nessa wants David to father a baby for her and Sam.

A. In scene 1, Nessa has talked to David about one of his patients, who bothers him with incessant phone calls. She has suggested that David tell the patient about a feminist collective that might solve her problems, and David has told her that some aspects of the women's movement are "a real turn-off."

> NESSA: So what if there are things that aren't, like, "tasteful." And any movement is gonna attract fucked-up people as well as strong, healthy, intelligent people, and some who would've been sympathetic are turned off. Well so fucking what. They'll be part of the second wave. I mean, you know this, David, any movement is going to alienate people who are too lazy to look at the main intentions of the movement. And I'll tell you something. I came out because I was sick and tired of being a "sympathizer." (*Pause.*) It's the only way. I really believe that. Women have been oppressed for so long that nothing is going to change if we keep sleeping with our oppressors. I'm sorry, but it's true.

B. In scene 2, Jim is talking to Doe as he considers Nessa's request to be the father of her child. He is reminiscing about the time when they were all in the country trying to beat a snowstorm, and he and David and their friend Chad were chopping wood for the fireplace.

> JIM: We were splitting and stacking and yelling and cursing and telling stories, and then the work itself—the physical labor—together with being out in that day—kind of overtook us. And we just kept going, lifting and splitting and lifting and splitting, in silence. Just our breath and the chopping and throwing and the sounds of the woods . . . And when we'd done half of it, we hopped into the truck and drove the rest up to our place and went at it there . . . And I was panting and aching and soaked with sweat—I had no idea where the strength was coming from to lift the ax. At one point I straightened up and just stood there.

3
Southern U.S. Regional Accents

Southern U.S. accents can be divided into four broad areas, and almost endlessly subdivided:

1. East Coast Southern (parts of Maryland, the rural areas around Tidewater Virginia, coastal North and South Carolina, coastal Georgia, north Florida);
2. Mid-Southern (West Virginia, southwest Virginia and the Appalachian Mountains, Kentucky, Tennessee);
3. Deep Gulf Southern (inland Georgia, inland North Carolina, inland South Carolina, Mississippi, Alabama, Louisiana)—these are the accents useful in most plays by Tennessee Williams;
4. West or Plains Southern (Missouri, Texas, Oklahoma, Arkansas).

The accents of many people from northern Virginia sound more Northern than Southern, but in the rural areas around the Tidewater, in southwest Virginia, and in the Appalachian areas of Virginia and West Virginia, as well as in the rural areas of Maryland, the accent is more strongly Southern; that is, we hear typical vowel and diphthong shifts away from General American.

In the Southwestern states of Arizona, Nevada, and New Mexico, General American with a Midwestern hard /r/ is the usual accent, and these states are therefore not classified as having Southern accents. In New

Mexico, more than in Arizona, there is a Spanish- and Navajo-influenced accent in which the /r/ is particularly hard, and the jaw somewhat tighter, with the mouth somewhat more closed than in General American, similar to the use of the mouth muscles in the Midwest.

There are many films in which you can hear authentic Southern accents, all of which are excellent models to follow. Actors from Texas who use their natural accents when their roles demand it include Sissy Spacek, Rip Torn, and Tommy Lee Jones. Geraldine Page was from Missouri: see her in the 1961 film version of Tennessee Williams's *Summer and Smoke*. Morgan Freeman is from Memphis, Tennessee; use his light accent as a model: see *Driving Miss Daisy* (1989) and *The Shawshank Redemption* (1994). Lane Smith's Memphis accent is heavier: see him in *My Cousin Vinny* (1992). And for an even broader Tennessee accent, listen to Dolly Parton in *9 to 5* (1980). Miriam Hopkins was from Georgia—you can hear light Southern touches in her performance as the aunt in the 1949 film *The Heiress*. For Savannah, Georgia, accents, see *Midnight in the Garden of Good and Evil* (1997). And you can hear the Mississippi accent of Elvis Presley in his many films.

For a refined Charlotte, North Carolina, accent, listen to the speeches of the Reverend Billy Graham. President Bill Clinton has an Arkansas accent, while James Garner has touches of his Oklahoma pronunciation. President Jimmy Carter speaks with the accent of Plains, Georgia; the accents associated with other towns in Sumter County are different from that of Plains, showing the amazing variety of Georgia accents.

Teach Yourself Southern U.S. Accents

Here is a summary of the important phonetic similarities in Southern accents:

1. **Consonant cluster reduction:** When more than one consonant is pronounced together, as in the phrase *hold fast*, the final consonant

of each word is often dropped: /HOHL FAS/. This is true of rural Southern speech generally—Alabama, Georgia, and Mississippi—but not necessarily of educated urban speakers.

2. **The Southern drawl:** While by no means ubiquitous, the Southern drawl does exist, especially in rural areas. Vowels and diphthongs are lengthened beyond what is usual in General American, and such lengthened, stressed syllables are spoken on a higher pitch.

3. **The ubiquitous shift from /I/ to /ah/:** The last part of the diphthong /I/ is dropped, and only the first part, /ah/, pronounced, sometimes as /ah/, sometimes as /a/. This phenomenon seems to be slowly changing, certainly in upper-class Southern speech. /I/ often retains a slight diphthongization before /d/, /k/, /m/, /n/, /p/, and /t/. In southwestern North Carolina, /I/ is often pronounced /a/. When unstressed, /I/ can also be pronounced as a schwa.

4. **The shift from /ih/ to /e/:** This shift is common in almost all Southern accents, so *pin* is pronounced /PEN/, and *tin* /TEN/. The vowel /ih/, shifting to /e/, also sometimes heard before /d/, /t/, /g/, and /k/, is also often diphthongized, with a schwa inserted between the vowel and the final consonant.

5. **The shift from /e/ to /ih/:** This shift is common in almost all Southern accents, so *pen* is /PIHN/, *anyway* is /IH nee WAY/, and *Memphis* is /MIHM fihs/. The vowel /e/, shifting to /ih/, also sometimes heard before /d/, /t/, /g/, and /k/, is also often diphthongized, with a schwa inserted between the vowel and the final consonant, in Tennessee and Texas for example, where *pen* shifts to /PEEuhN/, and *condemn* to /kuhn DEEuhM/.

In addition to the information just above, the following is essential:

1. **Positioning, placement, and use of the muscles of the mouth during speech:** The important general position for Southern accents

is with the mouth fairly open and the jaw loose. The tongue wants to rest at the bottom of the mouth.

2. **The sounds of /r/:** When an /r/ is pronounced it is hard, with the back of the tongue tensed and the tip curled farther back than in General American:

   a. **Non-rhotic with post-vocalic (after a vowel) /r/ dropped:** Most East Coast Southern; some Deep Gulf Southern (coastal Alabama, Mississippi, Louisiana).

   b. **Rhotic with post-vocalic (after a vowel) /r/ pronounced:** Some Deep Gulf Southern (inland Alabama, inland Georgia); West or Plains Southern; Mid-Southern. Even when the accent is rhotic, in unstressed syllables /r/ is sometimes not pronounced: *The other thing about living here* /thee U thuh theng uh BOWT LIH vihng HEER (alternatively, HEE uhr)/ (inland Georgia). And the /r/ in the accents of Birmingham, Alabama, and other cities is in the form of r-influenced vowels, rather than a strongly pronounced post-vocalic /r/.

3. **Vowels and diphthongs:** Vowels are often diphthongized, and the semi-vowel /y/ is sometimes inserted, resulting in a triphthong: *glance* becomes /GLAYuhNTS/, *glass* becomes /GLAYuhS/. This is true of inland Georgia, where the diphthongization is long, and of Texas, where the diphthongization is short. But diphthongs are often lengthened or drawn out, giving a kind of music to Southern accents, often called a Southern drawl, the word *drawl* itself being pronounced with a very long diphthong; in Alabama, you would hear the word *drawl* pronounced /DROHL/, with the /oh/ of sustained duration.

   a. **The sound of /ah/:** In such words as *department* and *father*, /ah/ is often heard as /aw/: /dih PAWT mihnt/, /FAW thuh/.

   b. **The shift from /aw/ to /oh/:** The vowel /aw/ in *because*, *bought*, *daughter*, *law*, and *thought* is often diphthongized as /OH/: /bih KOHZ/, /BOHT/, /DOH duh (with a tapped /d/)/, /LOH/,

/THOHT/. This is common in Alabama, inland Georgia, and the other Deep Gulf accents.

c. **The shift from /e/ to /ay/:** /e/ before /zh/, as in *leisure, measure,* and *pleasure,* is diphthongized and pronounced almost like /ay/ in *say* in rhotic Southern accents, as in Missouri and parts of Texas, but like the /e/ in *met* elsewhere.

d. **The sounds of /oh/:** /OH/ in *home* is much the same as in the North, but in coastal Maryland and the southern part of North Carolina it is often heard as /Oooh/ (with the /o/ in *work* as the first half of the diphthong) instead of /Oooh/ (with the /o/ in *not* as the first half of the diphthong). *Home* is pronounced /HOoohm/, *know* shifts to /NOooh/. (Note: This is also characteristic of a number of Northern accents, such as those heard in Philadelphia, Baltimore, and southern coastal New Jersey [the Pine Barrens], which are all rhotic accents.) /OH/ is also pronounced /UHooh/ and /Uooh/ in southern Virginia and northern North Carolina, so *château* is pronounced /sha TUHooh/ or /sha TUooh/, sometimes with an even stress on both syllables. The General American pronunciation is simply /sha TOH/.

e. **The shift from /oh/ to the schwa /uh/:** In words ending with the spelling "ow" or the pronunciation /oh/, a schwa is often substituted for the General American pronunciation /oh/, as in the word *fellow* /FEL uh/.

f. **The sounds of /o/ and /oy/:** The sound in "er" and "or" in the spelling of *fern* and *work* is sometimes pronounced /UHee/: /FUHeeN/, /WUHeeK/. The word *fur* is pronounced /FUH/ or, alternatively, /FU/. In Alabama and South Carolina these sounds are pronounced with an /oy/, which is very short here: /FOYN/, /FOY/, /WOYK/. In various areas of the South, including coastal Virginia, inland Georgia, and as far west as Alabama, Louisiana, and New Orleans, /oy/ is pronounced /aw/, thus losing its quality as a diphthong: *boil* /BAWL/, *oil* /AWL/, *spoil* /SPAWL/. In Alabama and inland Georgia /o/ also replaces /u/, so *of*, *but*, *other*, and *love* are pronounced /OV/, /BOT/, /O thuh/, and /LOV/.

g. **The sounds of /ow/:** In Deep Gulf and Mountain accents this diphthong often shifts to a flat, lengthened /Eooh/, so *grounds* is pronounced /GREoohndz/. The /e/ is close to being the diphthong /ay/.

h. **The sounds of /yooh/:** The diphthong /yooh/ (spelled "u" and "you") in unstressed final syllables is almost always pronounced with a schwa: *continue* is pronounced /KUN tihn yuh/ or /kun TIHN yuh/, *volume* is /VOL yuhm/. After a consonant, /yooh/ is almost always pronounced in all Southern accents, and some-times lengthened, as in the words *duke* and *news*: /DYOOHK/, /NYOOHZ/. In rural Southern speech, /yooh/ is often pronounced with a lengthened vowel /ee/ replacing the semi-vowel /y/ after a consonant: *duke* /DEEoohK/, *news* /NEEoohZ/. Pronounce this sound with the mouth closed and the lips protruded.

4. **Other consonants:**

   a. **Consonant cluster reduction:** An important phenomenon in many parts of the South is "consonant cluster reduction" in such combinations as "st," "ld," and "nd" at the ends of words. Examples: *host* /HOHS/, *hold* /HOHL/, *end* /IHN/. *My host told me there wasn't going to be a band* sounds like /MAH HOHS TOHL mee thay wudn gawna BEE uh BAN (alternatively, BAYuhN)/. In mountain ac-cents, especially when speech is slurred, some medial consonants are dropped, so *everybody* is pronounced /ER BAH dee/ or, more distinctly, /EV ruh BAH dee/. This is true for the Ozarks and parts of Texas. Note that the tapped /d/ in /dee/ is often heard. See p. 17 for how a tapped /d/ is articulated.

   b. **Final /g/-dropping:** The final /g/ in "-ing" endings is often dropped in lower-class Southern accents: *I was just going along* /AHZ js GOHN LAWNG/. Notice, too, the dropping of initial /w/ and the vowel /u/ in *was*, the absence of a vowel in *just*, and the dropping of /a/ in *along*. In the phrase *going to*, the final /g/ is sometimes dropped, as is the /t/ in *to*, and the final syllable of *going* is sometimes nasalized: *I'm going to go now* /ahm awn GOH now/.

c. **The sound of /h/:** In old-fashioned rural Southern accents, an /h/ is sometimes inserted in words beginning with /ih/, as in *it*, which becomes /hiht/. *It's true* /hihs TROOH/. /H/ is also pronounced by older Southerners in such words as *what* and *which* /HWAHT/, /HWIHCH/; but this /h/ has disappeared in the speech of younger Southerners: /WAHT/ or /WUHT/, /WIHCH/.

d. **The sounds of /l/:** /l/ is sometimes dropped in the middle of a word: *help* /HEP/, *wolf* /WOOF/. /l/ is sometimes sounded like /y/: *million* /MIH yuhn/, *a million dollars* /uh MIH yuhn DAH luhz/.

e. **The shift of /s/ to tapped /d/; dropped /s/:** The letter "s," pronounced as the voiced consonant /z/ in General American as in *isn't* and *wasn't*, is often heard as a soft /d/: /IHD nt/, /WU dnt/. This is heard in Texas, but also in many other parts of the South. The final /t/ is either very soft or else dropped altogether: /IH dn/, /WU dn/. Alternatively, the /d/ is dropped and the final /t/ pronounced: /IHNT/ or /EHNT/, /WUNT/; *It isn't true* /ih dehn TROOH/, with the /d/ tapped. Sometimes the final /t/ is dropped: /IHN/, /WUN/. These phenomena can all be heard from the same speaker at various times.

f. **The sounds of /t/:** The /t/ in Southern mountain speech, such as in the Ozarks and other parts of Arkansas, is often heard as a glottal stop (phonetic symbol: /?/) in the middle of words: *settler* /SE? lah/, *battle* /BA? l/ (much like the Bronx pronunciation). In rural Georgia and Alabama the spelling combination "t" and "y," where one word ends in "t" and the next one begins with "y" (as in *put you* [General American pronunciation: /POOT yooh/]) varies from the distinct standard pronunciation to the lower-class /POO chooh/. The word *temperature* is pronounced /TEM puh chuh/ in Missouri, Mississippi, and elsewhere in the South. In Deep Gulf

accents the spelling combination "t" and "h" in *right here* is pronounced /rah CHYUH/. *I'm going to put you right here* sounds like
/AHM awn POO chuh rah CHYUH/. Notice the dropping of initial
and final /g/ in *going*—very rural, very lower class.

g. **The sounds of /th / th/:** Voiced /th/ becomes /v/: *breathe* is
/BREEV/. Voiceless /th/ in lower-class Southern speech is often
heard as /f/: *both* is /BOHF/, *both of them* /BOHF u bm/, or /BOHF
u vm/, or /BOHF um/.

Intonation and Stress: The Music and Rhythm of the Accents

The pitch patterns or intonation of Southern speech gives these accents
characteristic and varied music. The lengthening of diphthongs changes
the rhythm of a sentence from that of General American by introducing
falling and rising tones on the lengthened diphthongs. There is also a
characteristic rising tone at the end of a declarative sentence, as if it were
a question.

Many words are stressed on the first syllable in all Southern accents,
whereas General American stresses the second syllable. Examples include
cement, *December*, *hotel*, *insurance*, *July*, and *Detroit*. The word *dispute* is
often stressed on the first syllable when it is a noun and on the second
syllable when it is a verb.

Teach Yourself the Traditional Accent of Charleston, South Carolina

For non-Southern actors, this is one of the simplest Southern accents to do,
and it is the accent many non-Southerners actually think of as classically
Southern. Charleston diction is very clear. For a perfect example of the
old-fashioned Charleston accent, listen to former Senator Ernest "Fritz"
Hollings in a YouTube interview at the South Carolina Book Festival. The
main phonetic points of the accent are as follows; note that 3b, 3e, and

3f give the accent its Charleston particularity, and that not doing these sounds will give you a General Southern East Coast accent:

1. **Positioning, placement, and use of the muscles of the mouth during speech:** The jaw is fairly loose, the lips very slightly protruded, and the accent feels slightly forward in the mouth.

2. **The sound of /r/:** The accent is largely non-rhotic, so post-vocalic /r/ is usually not pronounced, although before another consonant it is sometimes heard; this /r/ is very light: *thirty* /THOR dee/, with a tapped /d/ in the last syllable; *worse* /WORS/. But the linking /r/ usual in non-rhotic accents is largely absent, so instead of *for example* /faw ruhg ZAM puhl/, you hear /faw ihg (alternatively, eg) ZAM puhl/.

3. **Vowels and diphthongs:** The vowels and diphthongs are those of General American, with the following differences:

   a. **The shift of /ah/ to /aw/:** In Charleston, /ah/ shifts to /aw/, so *on* is pronounced /AWN/, and *want* is /WAWNT/.

   b. **The shift of /ay/ to lengthened /e/:** This is only occasional, and such words as *face* are sometimes pronounced not as /FAYS/ but as /FES/.

   c. **The shift of /I/ to /ah/:** The General American vowel /I/ usually shifts to /ah/, but before some consonants /I/ is heard as a lengthened diphthong: *time* /TIM/.

   d. **The shifts from /ih/ to /e/ and /e/ to /ih/:** These shifts, mentioned previously, are largely absent in Charleston, although they are sometimes heard, as in the words *anyway* /IH (alternatively, e) nee WAY/ and *example* /ihg (alternatively, eg) ZAM puhl/.

   e. **The occasional shift of /oh/ to short /aw/:** In such words as *coat* and *goat*, the diphthong is sometimes heard as /aw/: /KAWT/, /GAWT/. Note that this shift is only occasional.

   f. **The occasional shift of /ow/ to /oh/:** As in the Canadian pronunciation of such words as *house*, *out*, and *outstanding*, the diphthong

/ow/ is sometimes raised to become /oh/: /HOHS/, /OHT/, /oht STAN dihng/.

4. **Other consonants:**

   a. **The sound of /th / th/:** The initial /th/ in such words as *that* and *the* is often heard as /d/. In the middle of a word, /th/ is often heard as a tapped /d/: *other* /U duh/. The sound of /*th*/ in such words as *thing* and *think* is correctly pronounced.

   b. **The tapped /d/:** A tapped /d/ is usual, as it is in General American, in which /t/ or /d/ occur in the middle of such phrases as *state elections* /STAY dee LEK shuhnz/ or *needy folk* /NEE dee FOHK/; note that here /oh/ does not shift to /aw/.

   c. **Consonant cluster reduction:** Final consonants in consonant clusters are dropped; so, for example, *hold* is pronounced /HOL/ and *fast* is pronounced /FAS/.

Intonation and Stress: The Music and Rhythm of the Accent

The information on pitch given previously on Southern accents in general also applies to the Charleston accent, including the non-standard stressing on first syllables of certain words, such as *hotel* and *insurance*.

Practice Exercises

1. *I got a good look at you, and you're going to go to town. But you're never going to make it.*

Kentucky, Tennessee, but also Alabama and rural generally: /ah GAH duh good LOO kih chooh en yooh awn GOH de TAoohN / BCHOOH nih vawn MAY keet/

2. *I slept on the train.*

Educated General East Coast Southern, including North Carolina, Georgia; Texas: /ah SLIHPT awn thuh TRAYN/

Kentucky, Tennessee, but also Alabama and rural generally: /ah SLIHP (alternatively, SLEP) aw nuh TRAYN/

Notes: The diphthong /ay/ in the word *train* is lengthened, and is especially long in Texas speech. There is sometimes a rising note on the word *train*, making the declarative sentence sound like a question. In southwestern North Carolina, the pronoun *I* might be pronounced /a/.

3. *I'm going to tell you something, fellow. Don't mess with me. He got into a dispute. It was awful.*
General East Coast, Kentucky, Tennessee: /ahm GAW nuh (alternatively, AWN) TIHL (alternatively and rarely, TEL) yooh SUM *thi*hn (alternatively, SOM ?m, or SUM ?n) FE luh / DOHN MIHS wuh*th* mee / hee GAH DIHN tu DIHS pyooht / iht wuhz AW fl/
Alabama: /ahm ohn TIHL yooh SOM *thn* (alternatively, SOM ?m) FE luh / DOHN MIHS wuh*th* mee (alternatively, uh*th* mee) / hee GAH DIHN tu DIHS pyooht / iht wuhz OH fl/
Texas: /ahm GAW nuh TIHL yihooh SOM *then* FE luh / DOHN MEuhs wih*th* MEE / hee GAH DIHN tu DIHS pyooht / iht wuhz AW fl/

Notes: You will notice the shortening of *into a* to /IHN tu/. To pronounce /yooh/ the Southern way, just close your mouth and protrude the lips slightly.

4. From Mark Twain's *The Adventures of Tom Sawyer* (1876), chapter 1: "Y-o-u-u Tom—Aunt Polly Decides Upon Her Duty—Tom Practices Music—The Challenge—A Private Entrance"

The orphaned Tom Sawyer is being brought up by his mother's sister, Polly, who has a son of her own, Sidney. Tom has been playing hooky and has gone swimming, against Aunt Polly's orders. The novel takes place in a small town in Missouri, and you can practice this with a light non-rhotic Southern accent.

While Tom was eating his supper, and stealing sugar as opportunity offered, Aunt Polly asked him questions that were full of guile, and very deep—for she wanted to trap him into damaging revealments. Like many other simple-hearted souls, it was her pet vanity to believe she was endowed with a talent for dark and mysterious diplomacy, and she loved to contemplate her most transparent devices as marvels of low cunning. Said she:

"Tom, it was middling warm in school, warn't it?"

"Yes'm."

"Powerful warm, warn't it?"

"Yes'm."

"Didn't you want to go in a-swimming, Tom?"

A bit of a scare shot through Tom—a touch of uncomfortable suspicion. He searched Aunt Polly's face, but it told him nothing. So he said:

"No'm—well, not very much."

The old lady reached out her hand and felt Tom's shirt, and said:

"But you ain't too warm now, though." And it flattered her to reflect that she had discovered that the shirt was dry without anybody knowing that that was what she had in her mind. But in spite of her, Tom knew where the wind lay, now. So he forestalled what might be the next move:

"Some of us pumped on our heads—mine's damp yet. See?"

Aunt Polly was vexed to think she had overlooked that bit of circumstantial evidence, and missed a trick. Then she had a new inspiration: "Tom, you didn't have to undo your shirt collar where I sewed it, to pump on your head, did you? Unbutton your jacket!"

The trouble vanished out of Tom's face. He opened his jacket. His shirt collar was securely sewed.

"Bother! Well, go 'long with you. I'd made sure you'd played hookey and been a-swimming. But I forgive ye, Tom. I reckon you're a kind of a singed cat, as the saying is—better'n you look. *This* time."

She was half sorry her sagacity had miscarried, and half glad that Tom had stumbled into obedient conduct for once.

But Sidney said: "Well, now, if I didn't think you sewed his collar with white thread, but it's black."

"Why, I did sew it with white! Tom!"

But Tom did not wait for the rest. As he went out at the door he said: "Siddy, I'll lick you for that."

Charleston, South Carolina, Practice Exercises

1. *On the face of it, it's an idea whose time has come. For example, there has to be a winner and a loser.*
/awn duh FES uh viht ihs an ah DEEuh (alternatively, I DEEuh) hoohz TIM haz KUM / faw ihg ZAM puhl de HAS tuh bee uh WIH nuh an uh LOOH zuh/

2. *Let me turn just briefly to the issue before this House, because I take it this Board didn't do that and that assumes that you don't know what the facts are offhand.*
/LE mee TORN jihst BREEF lee tuh dee IH shooh bih faw dihs HOHS bih KAWZ ah tayk iht dihs BAWD DIH dn dooh dat n da duh SOOHMZ duht yooh daw NOH WUHT duh FAKS aw awf HAN/

Notes: The /d/ sounds in the syllables /dee/, /dihs/, /dat/, /da/, /duh/, and /daw/ are all tapped. The word *issue* could also be pronounced /IH shuh/, a typical Gulf States and Tennessee pronunciation as well as a Texas one. The /t/ in *that* can either be tapped or articulated very strongly.

Inland Georgia Practice Exercises

1. *Pay attention! I'm going to put that pot on the stove and add some olive oil.*
/PAY uh TIHN chuhn / AHM awn POOT that PAH daw nuh STOHV an AYD som AH leev AWL/

Notes: The /d/ in the syllable /daw/ is tapped. Note the shift from /a/ to /ay/ in the word *add*, and the /ee/ in the second syllable of *olive*.

2. *It's going to be delicious. Y'all're going to love it.*
/ihs GAW nuh bee dih LIH shuhs / YAWL uh GUH nuh LOV iht/

Texas Practice Exercises

1. *I don't care what they say, I think he's a dope.*
/ah dohn KAYuhR wut (alternatively, w*o*t) thay say / ah *th*enk heez uh
DOHP/

Note: The /d/ in *don't* is tapped, and the /n/ is nasalized.

2. *Far out on the range the cowboys ride on their horses.*
/faw RAooh dawn thuh RAYNJ thuh KAooh BAWeez RAHD awn ther
HAWR seez/

Notes: The /d/ in the syllable /dawn/ is tapped. Pay attention to the lengthening of the diphthongs.

Monologues

1. From Tennessee Williams's *A Streetcar Named Desire* (1947), Scene 2

The play is set in New Orleans, but the troubled Blanche DuBois and her
sister, Stella, are from Belle Reve, their plantation in Mississippi. (The
name means "Beautiful Dream," and the pronunciation, which in French
is /bel REV/, is anglicized to /BEL REEV/, which rhymes with the French
word for riverbank, *rive*.) Blanche, the Southern belle with a lurid past,
has been evicted from the estate and gone to live in Laurel, Mississippi,
before going to stay with her sister, who is married to Stanley Kowalski.
He is examining a box of her papers, convinced that Blanche is cheating
Stella out of her part of their inheritance.

The classic 1951 movie stars Marlon Brando, reprising his Broadway role
as the defensive, sadistic Stanley; Vivien Leigh as an ethereal Blanche; and
Kim Hunter, forthright and strong as Stella.

BLANCHE: [. . .] There are thousands of papers, stretching back over hundreds of years, affecting Belle Reve, as, piece by piece, our improvident grandfathers and father and uncles and brothers exchanged the land for their epic fornications—to put it plainly! (*She removes her glasses with an exhausted laugh*) The four-letter word deprived us of our plantation, till finally all that was left—and Stella can verify that!—was the house itself and about twenty acres of ground, including a graveyard, to which now all but Stella and I have retreated. (*She pours the contents of the envelope on the table*) Here all of them are, all papers! I hereby endow you with them! Take them, peruse them—commit them to memory, even! I think it's wonderfully fitting that Belle Reve should finally be this bunch of old papers in your big, capable hands!

2. From Tennessee Williams's *Cat on a Hot Tin Roof* (1955), Act 2

This play, Williams's personal favorite, takes place on the Mississippi Delta plantation of the Pollitt family, ruled with an iron hand by Big Daddy. Its story revolves around the dysfunctional relationship of Big Daddy's son Brick, a closeted homosexual, and his wife, Maggie. The family has gathered from near and far for Big Daddy's birthday celebration. Maggie is wary of Gooper Pollitt and his wife, Mae, who might edge Brick out of his inheritance, so Maggie pretends to be pregnant. Skipper, Brick's friend, has committed suicide.

The 1958 film stars Paul Newman as Brick and Elizabeth Taylor as Maggie, with Burl Ives as an impressive Big Daddy.

BRICK: Frig Mae and Gooper, frig all dirty lies and liars!—Skipper and me had a clean, true thing between us!—had a clean friendship, practically all our lives, till Maggie got the idea you're talking about. Normal? No!—It was too rare to be normal, any true thing between two people is too rare to be normal. Oh, once in a while

he put his hand on my shoulder or I'd put mine on his, oh, maybe even, when we were touring the country in pro-football an' shared hotel-rooms we'd reach across the space between the two beds and shake hands to say good-night, yeah, one or two times we—
[BIG DADDY: Brick, nobody thinks that that's not normal.]
BRICK: Well, they're mistaken, it was! It was a pure an' true thing an' that's not normal!

3. From Tennessee Williams's *Orpheus Descending* (1957), Act 1, Scene 2

Williams wrote that this play, a retelling of the Orpheus myth, is "the tale of a wild boy [Val, with his guitar] who wanders into a conventional community of the South [in a small Mississippi town] and creates the commotion of a fox in a chicken coop."

The 1959 film version, starring Marlon Brando, is titled *The Fugitive Kind*.

VAL: You know they's a kind of bird that don't have legs so it can't light on nothing but has to stay all its life on wings in the sky? That's true. I seen one once, it had died and fallen to earth and it was light blue colored and its body was tiny as your little finger, that's the truth, it had a body as tiny as your little finger and so light on the palm of your hand it didn't weigh more than a feather, but its wings spread out this wide but they was transparent, the color of the sky and you could see through them. That's what they call protection coloring. Camouflage, they call it. You can't tell those birds from the sky and that's why the hawks don't catch them, don't see them up there in the high blue sky near the sun!

4. From Beth Henley's *Crimes of the Heart* (1979)

Set in Hazlehurst, Mississippi, this is the story of the troubled, strange McGrath sisters, Meg, Lenny, and Babe. The youngest of the three, Babe, has shot her rich husband, Zackery, a state senator, and is out on bail and home in her kitchen. Willie Jay is a black fifteen-year-old, with whom

Babe had been having an affair. His dog (prosaically named Dog) has been adopted by Babe.

> BABE: All right then. Let's see . . . Willie Jay was over. And it was after we'd—
> [MEG: Yeah! Yeah.]
> BABE: And we were just standing around on the back porch playing with Dog. Well, suddenly, Zackery comes from around the side of the house. And he startled me 'cause he's supposed to be away at the office, and there he is coming from 'round the side of the house. Anyway, he says to Willie Jay, "Hey, boy, what are you doing back here?" And I said, "He's not doing anything. You just go on home, Willie Jay! You just run right on home." Well, before he can move, Zackery come up and knocks him once right across the face and then shoves him down the porch steps, causing him to skin up his elbow real bad on that hard concrete. Then he says, "Don't you ever come around here again, or I'll have them cut out your gizzard!" Well, Willie Jay starts crying, these tears come streaming down his face, then he gets up real quick and runs away with Dog following off after him. After that, I don't remember much too clearly, let's see . . . I went on into the living room, and I went right up to the davenport and opened the drawer where we keep the burglar gun . . . I took it out.

4
African-American Vernacular English (AAVE) Accents

African-American Vernacular English (AAVE), known by non-linguists as Black Street Speech or Ebonics, is a bona fide dialect with consistent grammatical features and a Southern-sounding accent. AAVE descends from rural Southern dialects, brought to the North during the Great Migration of the early twentieth century. Because of segregation, it persisted and evolved in the Northern cities, where accents were influenced by those surrounding it. There are thus older and newer varieties of Northern and Southern urban and rural AAVE.

In "African American Vernacular English: phonology" in *Varieties of English 2: The Americas and the Caribbean* (Mouton de Gruyter, 2008), Walter F. Edwards tells us that AAVE "is spoken most consistently by working-class African-Americans, particularly in urban areas . . . AAVE coexists with the colloquial [Standard American English] StAmE typically spoken [with the usual General American or regional accents] by middle-class African-Americans and middle-class whites."

An African-American dialect, Gullah, which some linguists include "under the umbrella of AAVE" ("African American Vernacular English: phonology"), is heard on the coastal islands off South Carolina and in the area around Charleston, as well as in Georgia and Florida, hence one of its other names: Sea Island Creole. It is also called Geechee, from the name the community of Gullah speakers gives to itself. You can hear examples of Gullah on YouTube.

Like AAVE, Gullah is non-rhotic, so post-vocalic (after a vowel) /r/ is not pronounced. In common with other Southern accents, Gullah drops prefixes and reduces consonant clusters: *I suppose so* is pronounced /ah SPOHZ soh/. *I expect so* is pronounced /ah SPEK soh/. The /l/ in the cluster "lp" is usually dropped, so *help* is pronounced /HEP/. There is also an occasional shift from /s/ to /sh/, particularly after the vowel /ih/ and before /t/. The word *restaurant*, for example, is pronounced /RIHSH trawn/, with the final /n/ nasalized; and *history* is pronounced /HIHSH tree/ or /HIHSH ree/, with the /t/ dropped.

Gullah has many fascinating grammatical differences from Standard American English. Among them are its own verb tenses: for instance, the past tense is indicated by the word *bin* (been): *I bin* [have been] *help* [helping] *them* /uh bihn HEP dem/. Past tense is also indicated by the word *done*: *I done show them that* /uh dun SHOW m (alternatively, dem) da? (alternatively, a?)/; this is also an AAVE characteristic. The continuous past is also shown by the word *binnuh*: *I binnuh show them* /u BIH nuh SHOH m/ (I have been showing them). The future tense is indicated by the word *gwine* (going to): *I gwine do that* /uh GWAHN dooh da? (alternatively, a?)/, with the /d/ tapped in both *do* and *that*. To learn more, see "Gullah: phonology" by Tracey L. Weldon in *Varieties of English 2: The Americas and the Caribbean*.

Versions of AAVE are used in stage plays by such brilliant, emotionally dynamic writers as August Wilson, Robert Alexander, Lorraine Hansberry, Lynn Nottage, Alice Childress, Jeff Stetson, Christopher Moore, Gloria Bond Clunie, Adrienne Kennedy, Shepsu Aakhu, and a host of other African-American playwrights.

There are many examples of AAVE in modern and contemporary films and television projects. See Spike Lee's *Do the Right Thing* (1989), *Mo' Better Blues* (1990), and *Malcolm X* (1992). And don't miss *Boyz n the Hood* (1991), directed by John Singleton, or *Hollywood Shuffle* (1987), a wry comedy about the stereotyping of African-Americans in Hollywood, co-written by, directed by, and starring Robert Townsend. Films in which you can hear a version of AAVE used by some characters include *Shaft* (1971), starring Richard Roundtree in the title role; and Melvin Van Peebles's *Sweet Sweetback's Baadasssss Song* (1971). Mario Van Peebles made a satirical semi-documentary about its making that is also a tribute to his father: *Baadasssss!* (2003)—the accents are mostly General American, but you will hear some touches of AAVE as well, from time to time. In the comedy *Madea's Family Reunion* (2006), written and directed by and starring Tyler Perry in multiple roles, the older generation speaks with an AAVE accent and touches of AAVE grammar, while the younger speaks StAmE with a General American accent. *Welcome Home, Roscoe Jenkins* (2008) and *Big Mommas: Like Father, Like Son* (2011), both comedies starring Martin Lawrence; *Dreamgirls* (2006), set in Detroit's music scene; and Lee Daniels's *Precious* (2009), about an abused, overweight New York City teenager, played by Gabourey Sidibe, with Mo'Nique as her mother, also provide examples of AAVE. And don't miss the documentary *That's Black Entertainment* (1989).

Teach Yourself AAVE Accents

1. **Positioning, placement, and use of the muscles of the mouth during speech:** The general position of the mouth muscles during speech, including the corners of the lips, is relaxed. The tongue is somewhat forward during speech, but remains relaxed. The accents "feel" as though they are pronounced in the middle of the mouth.

2. **The sound of /r/:** AAVE is characteristically non-rhotic, so postvocalic (after a vowel) /r/ is usually not pronounced. During pronunciation of an initial retroflex /r/, the back of the tongue is relaxed.

3. **Vowels and diphthongs:**
   a. **Substitution of /ih/ for /ee/ in word endings:** Often, although by no means always, a word ending orthographically in "y" /ee/ will be pronounced with an /ih/: *very* is pronounced /VE rih/; *very true*

is pronounced /VE rih TROOH/, or the /ih/ is dropped altogether. Note that this is an older phenomenon and is fast disappearing, although it is still heard among Southerners who are European-American, especially in Alabama, north Florida, and New Orleans.

b. **The diphthong /I/:** As in Southern accents generally, the second half of the /I/ diphthong is dropped. The pronoun *I* is pronounced /ah/.

c. **Reversal of /ih/ and /e/:** As in Southern accents generally, /ih/ and /e/ are reversed, so that *thing* is pronounced /THENG/ (and sometimes /THANG/) and *pen* is pronounced /PIHN/.

4. **Other consonants:**

a. **Reduction of consonant clusters:** Consonant clusters are often reduced, so you say /wuhs UP/ or even /SUP/, with the /p/ barely heard, for *what's up*; /PROB lee/, or even /PRAH lee/, for *probably*; /REG uh lee/ for *regularly*; /DOHN/, with the /n/ nasalized (the tongue does not press against the back of the gum ridge to complete the consonant), for *don't*; /LAS/ for *last*; /ek SEP/, or even /SEP/, for *except*, etc. The final /g/ in "-ing" endings is often dropped.

b. **The sound of /j/:** The combination /d/ and /y/ is often pronounced /j/, as in *did you*, heard as either /DIH jooh/, or /DIH juh/, or /JOOH/.

c. **The sounds of /ch/ and /sh/:** The combination /t/ and /y/ is often pronounced /ch/, as in *don't you*, heard as /DOHN chooh/, or /DOHN chuh/. Similarly, /sh/ is often heard is such words as *actually*: /AK shlee/.

d. **The sounds of /th / th/:** The /th/ in such words as *this* and *that* is often heard as a tapped /d/, but the voiceless /th/ in such words as *thing* is usually pronounced as /th/ at the beginning of a word. Sometimes in the middle and at the end of a word, especially in an older form of AAVE, voiceless /th/ is pronounced /f/ and voiced /th/ is eliminated in the context of a phrase, or replaced by a very soft /v/ or even /b/: the phrase *both of them* might be heard as /BOHF u vm (alternatively, bm, or um))/. Generally obsolete in present-day urban AAVE, the substitution of /f/ and /v/ is still often heard in contemporary rural Alabama and Mississippi accents, whether in the speech of African-Americans or European-Americans.

5. **Specific pronunciations:** *Ask* shifts to /AKS/, *grasp* shifts to /GRAPS/, *on* is pronounced /AWN/; words starting with /st/, such as *street*, are sometimes pronounced with /sk/: /SKREE?/, especially by younger speakers.

Intonation and Stress: The Music and Rhythm of the Accents

Although the intonation patterns are the same as in General American, there are more notes used in some AAVE patterns: Higher pitches and an up-and-down lilt can be quite common in situations where people are joking around or remonstrating with each other. A rise at the end of a statement is also common in such situations.

The stressing of initial syllables in certain words where General American stresses on later syllables is also usual; see the information on Southern accents in the previous chapter.

Practice Exercises

1. *What y'all be wantin' to do? It don't make no never mind.*
/wuh (alternatively, hwuh) CHAWL bee WAW?N nuh dooh / ih dohn MAYK noh NIH vah MAHN/

Notes: *Y'all*, a contraction of "you all," is a Southern expression meaning either "all of you" or "you," plural or singular. The /n/ sounds at the ends of the syllables /WAW?N/, /dohn/, and /MAHN/ are all nasalized, and barely heard; that is, the tongue does not complete the /n/ sound by applying pressure to the palate.

2. *What's up, bro? You jivin' me? I ain't going to do that. Yo, man, he's over there,*
if you looking for him. And don't you be asking him. She's not your gal. He was,
like, doing his thing for a while, know what I mean?
/wo SUP BROH / yooh JAH vihn MEE / ah ayn GAWN dooh da? / YOH man
heez OH vuh de fyooh LOOK ihn FAWM / an DOHN chooh bee AK sihn
ihm (alternatively, HEEuhm) / sheez NAH choh GAL / hee uhz lak DOOH
uhn ihz (alternatively, eez) *THANG faw WAHL NOH wuh dah MEEN/*

Notes: The phrase *What's up?* (sometimes spelled "wassup") is also frequently pronounced /SU?/ with a glottal stop, or /SUP/, with a barely
articulated /p/, and no *what* at the beginning. It is also modified to *What*
up? /wuh DUP/, with a tapped /d/. The /d/ sounds in the syllables /dooh/
and /da/ are tapped. The /n/ sounds in /ayn/ and /GAWN/ are nasalized.

3. *You can't hardly get there from here but you can get yourself right over from*
where you at.
/yuh (alternatively, yooh) KAYN HAW lee GIH de fm (alternatively, fruhm)
HEEuh buh chooh kihn GIH? choh SEF RAH DOH vuh fm WAY yooh a?/

Intonation pattern:

<pre>
                        get
You can't hardly
                    there from
                          here

                                              at
                right over
                        from where you
but you can get yourself
</pre>

Notes: The /d/ sound in the syllable /DOH/ is tapped. Notice the dropped
/l/ in *yourself*. The /n/ in the syllable /KAYN/ is nasal, and barely heard.

Notice the dropped /d/ in the word *hardly*. The /e/ in the syllable /de/ is long.

4. *They was like, yo, they really got on him, bro'. I had got off of the train, and there they was.*
/day wuhz lahk YOH day RIH lee GAH dawn eem BROH / ah had gah DAW fuh duh TRAYN an de (alternatively, e) day (alternatively, dee) WOZ/

Notes: The /d/ sounds in the second syllable /day/, and the syllables /dawn/, /DAW/, /duh/, /de/ (with a long vowel), and /day/ are all tapped.

Monologues

The accents in these excerpts are stage versions of AAVE rather than the full-out dialect, but the grammar and styles of speaking are enough to tell you that the characters are speaking with an AAVE accent.

1. From Lorraine Hansberry's *A Raisin in the Sun* (1958), Act 3

Walter Lee Younger, a disillusioned dreamer, is the protagonist of this seminal play about the prejudice experienced by a black family when they buy a house in a white Chicago neighborhood. Walter had wanted to invest his father's insurance money in a liquor store, with the help of his friend Willy Harris (an offstage character), who has proved to be less than honest in his business dealings.

In the 1961 film, Sidney Poitier played Walter, and Mama was played by Claudia McNeil.

> [MAMA: What you talking 'bout, son?]
> WALTER: Talking 'bout life, Mama. You all always telling me to see life like it is. Well—I laid in there on my back today . . . and I figured it out. Life just like it is. Who gets and who don't get. (*He sits down with his coat on and laughs.*) Mama, you know it's all divided up. Life is. Sure enough. Between the takers and the "tooken." (*He laughs.*)

I've figured it out finally. (*He looks around at them.*) Yeah, some of us are always getting "tooken." (*He laughs.*) People like Willy Harris, they don't never get "tooken." And you know why the rest of us do? 'Cause we all mixed up. Mixed up bad. We get to looking 'round for the right and the wrong, and we worry about it and cry about it and stay up nights trying to figure out 'bout the wrong and the right of things all the time . . . And all the time, man, them takers is out there operating, just taking and taking. Willy Harris? Shoot—Willy Harris don't even count. He don't even count in the big scheme of things. But I'll say one thing for old Willy Harris . . . He's taught me something. He's taught me to keep my eye on what counts in this world. Yeah—(*Shouting out a little*) Thanks, Willy!

2. From August Wilson's *Ma Rainey's Black Bottom* (1984), Act 1

One of August Wilson's earlier (and still best-known) plays, this is the third in *The Century Cycle*, also known as *The Pittsburgh Cycle*, a series of ten dramas that begins in 1900 and goes through the 1990s.

Ma Rainey's Black Bottom takes place in Chicago. Levee, a man in his early thirties, is a composer and one of the musicians who works with the famed blues singer Ma Rainey, who has come to a recording studio to lay down some tracks. She has experienced prejudice and discrimination, but Levee's experience of racism while growing up in Jefferson County, Mississippi, near Natchez, has been truly horrendous: He saw his mother raped in their home by a gang of white men when his father was away. His fellow band members, knowing nothing of this background, tease him for being subservient to the white producer, and for behaving with him in a "spooked up" way. This is part of his response, in the concluding speech of act 1.

LEVEE: [. . .] My daddy came back and acted like he done accepted the facts of what happened. But he got the names of them mens from Mama. He found out who they was and then we announced we was moving out of that county. Said goodbye to everybody . . . all the neighbors. My daddy went and smiled in the face of one of them crackers who had been with my mama. Smiled in his face and sold him our land. We moved over with relations in Caldwell. He got us settled in and then he took off one day. I ain't never seen him since. He sneaked back, hiding up in the woods, laying to get them eight or nine men. (*Pauses.*) He got four of them before they got him. They tracked him down in the woods. Caught up with him and hung him and set him afire. (*Pauses.*)

My daddy wasn't spooked up by the white man. Nosir! And that taught me how to handle them. I seen my daddy go up and grin in this cracker's face . . . smile in his face and sell him his land. All the while he's planning how he's gonna get him and what he's gonna do to him. That taught me how to handle them. So you all just back up and leave Levee alone about the white man. I can smile and say yessir to whoever I please. I got time coming to me.

3. Two Monologues from Alice Childress's One-Act Play *Wine in the Wilderness* (1969)

The scene is "a one room apartment in a Harlem Tenement." Tomorrow-Marie, called Tommy, is "a woman factory worker aged thirty," born in Baltimore and raised in Harlem, the famous, largely African-American area of New York City. She has come to the apartment of Bill Jameson, who is painting a triptych on black womanhood titled *Wine in the Wilderness*, and wants Tommy to be the subject of the third painting.

A. Here, Tommy tells Bill about some of the misgivings she had even before she met him.

TOMMY: I'm standin' there in the bar . . . tellin' it like it is . . . next thing I know they talkin' bout bringin' me to meet you. But you know what I say? Can't nobody pick nobody for nobody else.

It don't work. And I'm standin' there in a mis-match skirt and top and these sneaker-shoes. I just went to put my dresses in the cleaner . . . Oh, Lord, wonder if they burn down the cleaner. Well, no matter, when I got back it was all over . . . They went in the grocery store, rip out the shelves, pull out all the groceries . . . the hams . . . the . . . the . . . can goods . . . everything . . . and then set fire . . . Now who you think live over the grocery? Me, that's who. I don't even go to the store lookin' this way . . . but this would be the time, when . . . folks got a fella they want me to meet.

B. Bill has an ulterior motive for wanting to paint Tommy's likeness. He has not shared it with her, which makes her feel deceived and betrayed. She decides to leave.

TOMMY: I don't stay mad; it's here today and gone tomorrow. I'm sorry your feelins' got hurt, . . . but when I'm hurt I turn and hurt back. Somewhere, in the middle of last night, I thought the old me was gone . . . lost forever, and gladly. But today was flippin' time, so back I flipped. Now it's "turn the other cheek" time. If I can go through life other-cheekin' the white folk, . . . guess y'all can be other-cheeked too. But I'm going back to the nitty-gritty crowd, where the talk is we-ness and us-ness.

5
Caribbean Islands Accents

The accents of immigrants from the Anglophone Caribbean countries of the Bahamas, Trinidad, Jamaica, Barbados, and other islands are widely heard throughout the U.S., especially in large cities like New York.

The French Creole accents of Haiti are also ubiquitous. Shift /ih/ to /ee/: *bit* /BEET/; and do the consonant shifts suggested in chapter 8 on Canadian French, including the shift of /th / *th*/ to /d/ and /t/. Keep everything feeling forward, with strong consonants, and you will have the Haitian accent, heavy or light according to the character.

Listen to the musical *Once on This Island* (1990) by Lynn Ahrens and Stephen Flaherty; it is based on Caribbean legends. The plays of Nobel Prize–winning author Derek Walcott, from the Anglophone island of St. Lucia, are worth exploring as well; many of his works are set in the French Creole–speaking islands. He has explored and used the rich Caribbean folklore, also captured by playwrights for young actors in such books as Paloma Mohamed's *Caribbean Mythology and Modern Life: Five One-Act Plays for Young People* (The Majority Press, 2004), which has an introduction about the theater of Guyana, an Anglophone country on the Caribbean coast of South America. Caribbean theater has a rich tradition, exemplified in the works of Kendel Hippolyte, Dennis Scott, and Rawle Gibbons, whose popular masterwork is *A Calypso Trilogy*. And read British playwright Winsome Pinnock's evocative *Talking in Tongues* (1991), set partly in Jamaica.

There is a thriving Caribbean film industry, and hundreds of films to choose from to listen to the accents. A minuscule selection: from the Bahamas, the television series *Bahamas Mama* (2012), and *Float* (2007), a short drama about gay rights; from Jamaica, *Life and Debt* (2001), a documentary about globalization and its effects on Jamaican industry, and the documentary *RasTa: A Soul's Journey* (2011), about the granddaughter of Bob and Rita Marley, as she explores the roots of Rastafari in eight countries; and from Trinidad, the bacchanalian documentaries *Carnival Coming* (2011) and *Masquerade* (2011).

Teach Yourself Caribbean Islands Accents

There are some common phonetic characteristics that will enable you to do an authentic general accent, to which you can add specific sounds that will localize the accent.

1. **Positioning, placement, and use of the muscles of the mouth during speech:** The general position of the vocal apparatus is much the same as in General American. The position of the mouth muscles during speech, including the corners of the lips, is relaxed. The accents "feel" as though they are pronounced in the middle of the mouth.

2. **The sounds of /r/:** The accents of Barbados and Jamaica are rhotic, and post-vocalic /r/ is lightly pronounced. The accents of the Bahamas, Trinidad, and many Eastern Caribbean islands are non-rhotic. In all positions—beginning, middle, or end of a word—/r/ is always retroflex, with the bottom of the tongue curled slightly up toward the palate.

3. **Vowels and diphthongs:** Especially in important stressed syllables, vowels and diphthongs are lengthened. Many diphthongs shift to monophthongs (pure vowels).

a. **The sounds of /a/ and /ah/:** Substitute /ah/ for /a/, but make the /ah/ more closed; that is, lift the tongue slightly above its position for a broad, open-throated /ah/: *man* /MAHN/, *that* /DAHT/.

b. **The schwa /uh/ and /ih/ or /ah/:** Instead of a schwa /uh/ being used in unstressed syllables, /ih/ is used. Vowels in unstressed syllables remain strong. At the end of a word, /uh/ often shifts to /ah/, especially in the non-rhotic Caribbean accents: *over*, *power* /OH vah/, /POW wah/.

c. **The sound of /aw/:** The pure vowel /aw/ in such words as *law*, *talk*, and *walk* is long, but it often shifts to /ah/: *daughter* /DAH tah/, *law* /LAH/, *corn* /KAHN/ or /KYAHN/ (Jamaica).

d. **The shift of /ay/ to /e/ or /ee/:** The diphthong /ay/ shifts to a single lengthened vowel /e/: *say* /SE/. In Trinidad, /ay/ shifts to /ee/: *came* /KEEM/.

e. **Diphthongization of /e/:** In such words as *Mary* and *there*, a schwa and a /y/ are sometimes inserted, and the vowel /e/ shifts to /ee/: /MEEyuh ree/, /DEEyuhr/ or /DEEyuh/. This is heard in Barbados, Jamaica, and many other islands.

f. **The sound of /o/:** In such words as *got*, *hot*, and *not*, the short /o/ is used, as in British RP or Canadian English, although sometimes /ah/ is used, as in General American.

g. **The shift of /o/ to /e/:** In the non-rhotic Caribbean accents, in such words as *first*, *girl*, and *work*, the /o/ sometimes shifts to /e/: /FEST/, /GEL/, /WEK/.

h. **The sounds of /oh/ and /aw/:** This diphthong is composed of the short /o/ in *hot* (not the /u/ in *but*), the stressed half of the diphthong, and the /ooh/ in *boot*. In most Caribbean accents, it shifts to /aw/: *home* /HAWM/, with the vowel quite long. In Jamaica and Trinidad it is closed to become /ooh/: *home* /HOOHM/.

i. **The shift of /ow/ to /oh/:** In Trinidad, /ow/ often shifts to /oh/, as in Canadian English: *house* /HOHS/, *out* /OHT/.

j. **The sounds of /u/:** In most Caribbean accents, instead of /u/, /ah/ is used: *but* /BAHT/, *love* /LAHV/, *one* /WAHN/. In Jamaica, /u/ shifts to /o/, the short sound in *hot*: *above* /a BOV/, *but* /BOT/, *love* /LOV/.

k. **Insertion of /y/:** In Jamaica, this semi-vowel is often inserted after /k/ or /g/ before an /ah/: *car* /KYAH/, *garden* /GYAH dihn/.

4. **Other consonants:** Consonants are clear, well articulated, and hard; that is, the pressure of one articulator on another—for instance, the pressure of the tongue against the palate just behind the upper front teeth to form a /t/ or a /d/—is strong, often stronger than in General American or British RP.

    a. **Dropping or insertion of /h/:** Initial /h/ is regularly dropped, as in London accents. But in the Bahamas, /h/ is inserted into words where it does not ordinarily exist: *eggs* /HEGZ/, *hour* /HOWAH/.

    b. **The sounds of /l/:** For initial /l/, as in the word *like*, the tongue is slightly relaxed and its tip touches the gum ridge lightly. Very often a dark, liquid /l/ is heard in these accents, as opposed to the usual General American /l/.

    c. **The sounds of /th / th/:** These consonants often shift to /d/ or /t/, respectively: *mouth* /MOWT/, *three* /TREE/, *smooth* /SMOOHD/, *that* /DAHT/. And /th/ shifts to a tapped /d/ in the middle of a word: *other* /U dah/, *father* /FAH dah/.

    d. **Consonant cluster reduction:** The last consonant in a cluster is dropped. Final /t/ is dropped in word endings: *don't* /DAWN/, *last* /LAS/ or /LAHS/, *left* /LEF/. Final /d/ is dropped in such words as *hand* /HAN/.

    e. **Consonant devoicing:** In the Bahamas, final /z/ sounds are devoiced to /s/: *is* /his/, *buzz* /BAHS/.

5. The past participle *been* usually rhymes with *bean*.

Intonation and Stress: The Music and Rhythm of the Accents

One of the most important features of Caribbean accents is the pitch / intonation patterns, some of which you will find in the practice exercises.

In one Jamaican pattern, sentences begin on a high pitch and go step by step to a lower final pitch. Otherwise, the usual pattern of ending a declarative sentence on a falling tone and a question on a rising tone is followed.

In Trinidad, older speakers sometimes have an up-and-down lilt on every few words in a declarative sentence that goes up and down and then up again at the end.

Stress patterns are also very important in these accents. Whereas American and British stress is on the first syllable of such words as *celebrate* and *realize*, Caribbean stress is on the last syllable. In fact, the general tendency is to stress the penultimate syllable, giving these varieties of English their characteristic rhythm. A word like *accentuated*, stressed on the second syllable in both British RP and General American, has its primary stress in the Caribbean accents on the fourth syllable: /ak SEN tchooh AY tihd/. There is an even quality to the stress patterns of Caribbean accents, due to the tendency of not differentiating stressed and unstressed syllables, despite the lengthening of some vowels, so a word like *regular* is pronounced /RE GYOOH LAH (alternatively, LAHR)/, instead of General American /RE gyuh (alternatively, gyooh) luhr/.

Practice Exercises

1. *Oh, man, I think he's walking in the garden.*
/aw MAHN I TIHNK heez WAH king in dih GYAHR dihn/

Note: The pronunciation /GYAHR dihn/, with the merest suggestion of a /y/, is Jamaican; in other accents, such as that of Trinidad, it would be pronounced /GAH dihn (alternatively, den)/.

Jamaican Intonation (Pitch) Pattern:

Oh,
    man,
        I
           think
              he's
                 walking
                    in the
                        gar-
                           den.

Trinidad Intonation (Pitch) Pattern:

                        the   den.
        think he's
    man,   walking in   gar-
Oh,   I

2. *It's my sister, you know. She's on vacation. She goes places and calls me. She takes the car. My uncle goes, too, but he doesn't call me, man.*
/ihts mI SIHS tuhr yooh naw / sheez awn vay KE shn / shee GAWZ PLE sihz ahn KAWLZ (alternatively, KAHLZ) mee / shee TEKS dih KYAH / mI AHN kl GAWZ tooh baht ee DAHZ ihn KAWL (alternatively, KAHL) mee MAHN/

Notes: Notice the lengthened vowel /e/ in *vacation* and *places*, and the absence of the schwa in the last syllable of *vacation*. The /aw/ in *calls* is also lengthened. For Jamaica and Trinidad, pronounce the words *know* and *goes* with /ooh/: /NOOH/, /GOOHZ/.

General Caribbean, including Trinidad and Jamaica Intonation (Pitch) Pattern:

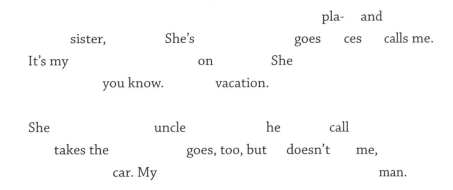

3. *So my family is against it, but I want to buy that building. With good tenants there it will pay for itself, man. It's a good investment, I tell you, man. It's right there, in my grasp.*

/saw ml FAM lee ihz ah GENST eet bah tI WAHN tooh BI daht BEEuhL dihng / wiht goohd TE nahnts DEE uhr iht wihl PE faw (alternatively, fah) riht SELF MAHN / eets ah GOOHD ihn VEST mihnt I TEL yooh MAHN / its RIT THAYuhR (alternatively, THEEuhR, or DEEyuhR) ihn ml GRASP/

Notes: All the /ih/ sounds are lengthened, and are sometimes as long as /ee/. Notice the dropping of the second syllable in *family*.

4. *Oh, you know, the beaches down here are gorgeous and there is always lots of sunshine and the food is delicious, nice and spicy sometimes, too, like I told you. But you can wash it all down with a nice glass of milk.*

/aw yooh naw dee BEE chihz down HEE rah GAW jus ahn DE rihz (alternatively, DEEuh rihz) AWL wez LAWTS (alternatively, LAWS) uv sun SHIN ahn dee FOOD eez dee LIH shus NI sahn SPI see sahm TIMZ tooh lIk I TAWL yooh / bu chooh kahn (alternatively, kan, or kn, with a nasal /n/) WAHSH (alternatively, WAWRSH) ih dahl down wee duh NIS GLAHS uh MIHLK (alternatively, MEEuhLK)/

Notes: The /d/ sounds in the syllables /dahl/ and /duh/ are tapped. Remember that vowels and diphthongs are long.

Monologues

1. From Derek Walcott's *Dream on Monkey Mountain* (1970), Prologue

Many of Derek Walcott's plays are set in a French-Creole milieu, and he often uses the Creole language. His stories generally involve Caribbean mythology and fantasy. This particular play concerns evolution, creation, and the ape-like qualities of man. On an unspecified "West Indian Island," Makak (the macaque) is put on trial and prosecuted by the authoritarian Corporal. The Creole French means, "Raise your head, you!" The word *ous* is a shortening of *vous* (you).

> CORPORAL: My noble judges. When this crime has been categorically examined by due process of law, and when the motive of the hereby accused by whereas and ad hoc shall be established without dychotomy, and long after we have perambulated through the labyrinthine bewilderment of the defendant's ignorance, let us hope, that justice, whom we all serve, will not only be done, but will appear, my lords, to have itself, been done . . . (*The* JUDGES *applaud*) Ignorance is no excuse. Ignorance of the law is no excuse. Ignorance of one's own ignorance is no excuse. This is the prisoner. I will ask the prisoner to lift up his face. *Levez la tête-ous*! [/luh vé lah TET OOH/]
>
> (MAKAK *lifts up his head. The* CORPORAL *jerks it back savagely.*)
> CORPORAL: My lords, as you can see, this is a being without a mind, a will, a name, a tribe of its own.

2. From Kendel Hippolyte's *The Drum-Maker: A Play in Three Movements* (1983), Movement 1

This play, set in Jamaica, is in the form of story-telling, with a narrator and actors who bring the drama to life.

NARRATOR: I want to tell you. I want to tell you in such a way that you cyah get to sleep a night-time. And if you sleep, I want to trouble your dream. I want you walking around in the daylight with your eyes red and full of hot sand, so that you cyah close dem. You dream too much. You sleep too dam' much. Me? I cyah sleep, Jack. Sake o' Jack, I cyah sleep. Him never mad though. Just see too much. I myself never see what him was saying till I start understand this network—and who make the net. But is a long time him trying to make me see. From I was a little boy and he have his house in the little village outside Moffat estate.

3. From Dennis Scott's One-Act Play *The Crime of Annabel Campbell* (1983)
Set in Jamaica, the play concerns a murder, and it portrays the lives of ordinary people. One of the individuals caught up in the horror of the situation is Angela, the housekeeper.

ANGELA: Lord it's hot outside, Bel. You haven't even touched them! Here, let me do it. I must look a mess, Bernie. The clock, set it to the right time, boy! Don't stand there! Oh, I'm dying of thirst! I'm getting old and lazy, I know that, there was a time I'd blow through a house and leave it clean as a whistle—lemonade, lemonade! That's what we need! Bel, darling, if you're determined to stand there dreaming of your Johnny, why don't you make us something cool to drink? Oh my Lord, how the day has flown! I can scarce believe it's almost four already! Here, hurry on, you're only getting in the way, and there's a million and one things to do.

4. From *Ten to One* (1999), the Third Play in Rawle Gibbons's *A Calypso Trilogy*, Prologue
These musical plays feature calypso dances of the 1950s and 1960s. Tants is a businesswoman.

[LULU: Tants, is true what the Doctor say about the white wicked-
ness in the days of slavery?]

TANTS: What stupidness you asking me, chile? For your information, I was never a slave and I have no doctorship in History. But
common sense alone tell me put a whip in any man hand and he
will use it. I watching this thing. That Dr. Paul and all of them who
jumping up at meeting is when they feel the whip on their back,
they will know who is the real massa. (*Melody and Blakie come along
the street with Second Spring in tow.*) Do fast, chile! Time to serve.
My customers coming, belly in hand.

6
Hispanic Accents

Spanish is the first language of four to five hundred million people in Spain, most Central and South American countries, and some Caribbean islands. It is also spoken nationwide in the U.S. New York and other urban areas are home to large Dominican and Puerto Rican populations, just as Arizona, New Mexico, California, and Texas are to Mexican-Americans and Florida is to its Cuban-American population.

The accents of the immigrant generations depend on the Spanish pronunciation of their places of origin. Many Latinos born or raised in the U.S. are perfectly bilingual in Spanish and Standard American English (StAmE). And many do not speak Spanish at all: Their mother tongue is StAmE, typically spoken with the usual General American or regional accents. There is also a distinctive Chicano English (ChcE) dialect and accent, which is not the speech of all Mexican-Americans.

Chicano /chih KA no/, a Mexican-Spanish word derived from the Spanish for Mexican, *mexicano* /ME khee KAH no/, refers to Americans of Mexican descent born in the U.S. As Otto Santa Ana and Robert Bayley tell us in "Chicano English: phonology" in *Varieties of English 2: The Americas and the Caribbean*, Chicano English is a bona fide dialect, not simply Spanish-accented English, as many non-linguists and even some linguists opine. In "Chicano English: morphology and syntax," the authors inform us, "Speakers of ChcE are concentrated primarily in the urban *barrios* [/BAH ree os/ (neighborhoods)] of California and the southwestern United States."

In films, you can hear Raul Julia, who had a very slight Puerto Rican Spanish accent, in *Kiss of the Spider Woman* (1985) and *Tequila Sunrise* (1988). Listen to Desi Arnaz for a Cuban accent in the *I Love Lucy* (1951–1957) television series. Leonard Bernstein's *West Side Story* requires Puerto Rican Spanish accents, and you can hear them in the 1961 film. Actor and comedian George Lopez, of Mexican-American background, is best known for his hit comedy series *George Lopez* (2002–2007); his accent is the General American of the California where he is from, but he can adopt a Chicano English accent when he pleases. Also from California is the hilarious actor and comedian Cheech Marin, who does a perfect Mexican-American accent, which is not his actual way of speaking, but he has made it his own. See him with Canadian actor Tommy Chong in *Cheech and Chong's Up in Smoke* (1978) and *Cheech and Chong's Next Movie* (1980). Listen to the recording of *In the Heights* (2008), by actor and Tony Award–winning composer Lin-Manuel Miranda and Quiara Alegría Hudes. This musical, the first by Hispanic-Americans to come to Broadway, concerns the Dominican-American community in Washington Heights, a neighborhood on the northern side of Manhattan. For more Mexican Spanish accents, see the delightful *Tortilla Soup* (2001), about a Mexican-American master chef and his three daughters. And don't miss the hilarious Rosie Perez, born in Brooklyn, whose Puerto Rican accent is perfect in *It Could Happen to You* (1994). Be sure to read the complex dramas and comedies of Luis Valdez about the Mexican-American experience, combating ethnic stereotypes; the exciting dramas of Puerto Rican playwrights José Rivera and Miguel Piñero; and the starkly emotional plays of Cuban-Americans Nilo Cruz and Maria Irene Fornes.

Teach Yourself Hispanic Accents

Most of the information given here applies to speakers whose first language was Spanish and who learned English as a second language. Also included is information on Chicano English and on the occasional Spanish-language influence heard in the accents of some Hispanic-Americans.

1. **Positioning, placement, and use of the muscles of the mouth during speech:** The general position of the mouth muscles during speech, including the corners of the lips, is relaxed. The accents "feel" as though they are pronounced more forward in the mouth than in General American. The lips are fairly loose and touch lightly to form such consonants as /b/ and /v/. The jaw is relaxed and half closed. Say *wah*, *wah*, *wah* several times in a row, and you will have the idea.

2. **The sound of /r/:** The /r/ in Spanish is trilled, usually receiving one tap, or, if doubled, two taps. You often hear a trilled /r/ in Spanish accents in English. Post-vocalic /r/ is pronounced. In Chicano English, the trilled /r/ is not used; the back of the tongue is tensed slightly, the tip is retracted as it curls upward, the sides of the tongue press lightly against the sides of the palate, and the lips are slightly forward when pronouncing the retroflex /r/.

3. **Vowels and diphthongs:** The vowel system in Spanish consists of /ah/, /e/, /ih/ (lengthened; spelled "i"), /o/, and /ooh/ (spelled "u"). The vowels have open and closed versions. Diphthongs often shift to pure vowels in a Spanish accent in English. In Chicano English, vowels, particularly in final syllables, are lengthened slightly, and the duration of the syllable is consequently sustained. Also in ChcE, diphthongs are often shifted to single vowels.

   a. **The shift of /aw/ to /ah/:** In Chicano English, the sound of /aw/ in such words as *law*, *talk*, and *walk* shifts to /ah/: /LAH/, /TAHK/, /WAHK/.

   b. **The shift of /e/ to /ay/:** In a Spanish or Chicano English accent, this shift is sometimes heard, so *pleasure* is pronounced /PLAY shuhr/.

   c. **The sounds of /ee/ and /ih/:** Substitute a lengthened /ee/ for both /ih/ and /ee/ in a Spanish accent. Alternatively, use the intermediate vowel /ih/; for its pronunciation, see the list of phonetic symbols used in this book.

d. **The shift of /oh/ to /aw/:** In a heavy Spanish accent, /oh/ shifts to a short /aw/, so *home* is pronounced /KHAWM/.

e. **The shift from /ow/ to /a/ or /ah/:** Especially among older speakers of Chicano English, the /ow/ in such words as *council*, *house*, and *town* shifts to /a/: /KAN sihl/, /HAS/, /TAN/. Younger speakers often say /ah/ in these words: *What are you talking about?* /wu dahr (alternatively, duhr) yooh TAH kihn uh BAHT/, with the /d/ in the syllable /dahr/ tapped and the /t/ at the end of *about* very lightly pronounced.

f. **The sounds of /y/:** This semi-vowel has various pronunciations in Spanish, which carry over into English. In Castilian Spanish, /y/ is like its English counterpart. In Argentina it sounds like /zh/, and in Puerto Rico and Cuba almost like the /j/ in *edge*. *Yo no se* (I don't know) is /yo no SE/ in Castilian, /zho no SE/ in Argentina, and /jo no SE/ in Puerto Rico. In Chicano English, initial /y/ is pronounced as /ch/: *you* /CHOOH/. The way this /y/ sound shifts to other sounds in the different Spanish accents is often the way it is pronounced in a heavy accent in English.

4. **Other consonants:** Consonants are well articulated and softer than in General American. Keep the lips slightly parted when articulating bilabial consonants, such as /b/ and /v/, which sound like each other in Spanish.

a. **The sounds of /ch/ and /j/:** The consonant /ch/ exists in Spanish, but usually only initially, so final /ch/ is sometimes heard as /sh/: *church* /CHORSH/. But be very careful not to overdo the substitution of /sh/ for /ch/, or you will sound like a caricature. The /j/ sound does not exist in Spanish, and /ch/ is often substituted for it, a characteristic especially strong in Chicano English: *edge* /ECH/, *stranger* /STREN chuhr/.

b. **The tapped /d/:** The tapped /d/, in which the tongue does not press strongly against the back of the gum ridge to form a hard /d/, is heard not only at the beginning of syllable in the middle of a word (see under /th/ *th*/), but also in consonant clusters, as in the word *didn't* /DIH dihnt/, where the tapped /d/ at the beginning of the second syllable is very lightly articulated. The General American pronunciation is /DIH dnt/, with only the slightest hint of a schwa between /d/ and /n/. A glottal stop may substitute for the final /t/; sometimes the final /t/ is dropped altogether, especially before another consonant: *I didn't know* /I DIH dih (alternatively, DIH ?ih) NOH/. The latter is sometimes heard in a New York City Hispanic-American accent, and is becoming usual in New York accents generally.

c. **The sound of /h/:** Although the letter "h" is used in Spanish orthography, the sound of /h/ does not exist in Spanish pronunciation, but the letters "j" and "x" are used to represent a soft /kh/. Substitute a soft /kh/ for initial pronounced /h/ in a Spanish or foreign Hispanic accent.

d. **The Spanish /l/:** The Spanish /l/ is pronounced with the tip of the tongue forward, just behind where the upper gum ridge opens up into the palate. This sound sometimes carries over into the accents of people whose first language is Spanish, or of some Hispanic-Americans; it is also sometimes heard in a New York City Hispanic-American accent.

e. **The sounds of /n/ and /ng/:** The /n/ at the end of a word is often heard as /ng/ in some accents of the Spanish language, particularly in Cuba and Puerto Rico. Sometimes /n/ is simply a nasalized vowel. The word *ten* in the Cuban or Puerto Rican accent in English of someone whose first language is Spanish is heard variously as /TENG/ or /TEN/, with the /n/ nasalized. The latter pronunciation is often heard in a Latino accent by someone who is bilingual and has grown up speaking both Spanish and English: *It's ten-twenty* /ihs TEN TWEN tee/, with the final /n/ nasalized. In Chicano English, *ten* and the syllable /TWEN/ would be lengthened slightly.

f. **The sounds of /th / th/:** Substitute /d/ and /t/ for /th/ and /*th*/; and a tapped /d/ for /th/ and for /t/ when the sounds occur between vowels: *other* /U duhr/, *matter* /MA duhr/. This is also the case in Chicano English. But /th/ and /*th*/ are often correctly pronounced, especially by educated speakers.

g. **The shift from final /z/ to /s/:** There is no /z/ sound in Spanish, although the letter is used in spelling. In South America it is pronounced /s/, and in Castilian Spanish, /*th*/. Otherwise /s/ in a Spanish accent and also in Chicano English is substituted for a /z/ in English, particularly at the end of a word. This is true even in some accents used by native-born Americans of Latino descent, where the sound is spelled with an "s": *please* /PLEES/, *says* /SES/, *does* /DUS/. But do not exaggerate this characteristic: Pronounce /s/ lightly, without dwelling on it.

h. **The sounds of /sh/ and /zh/:** Voiceless /sh/ often substitutes for the voiced /zh/, so that *measure*, for example, is pronounced /MAY shuhr/, especially in a heavy Spanish or Chicano English accent.

i. **Consonant cluster reduction:** As for so many Southern and urban accents, drop the final /d/ or /t/ in consonant clusters in words like *old*, *fast*, *last*, and *most*.

Intonation and Stress: The Music and Rhythm of the Accents

Mexican, Cuban, and Puerto Rican Spanish accents all have different intonation patterns, different kinds of music. These patterns can be carried over into an accent in English.

There is usually no problem for Spanish-speaking people in learning to stress English words correctly. We have to look to phonetics and pitch patterns for the characteristics that create a Spanish accent in English.

Chicano English often has more musical notes than other accents of English. And the lengthening of vowels in stressed syllables gives the accent its particular rhythm. For example, in the sentence *That is good* there may be a glide downward on the word *good*, and the vowel in that syllable may be lengthened: /da dihs GOOD/, with a tapped /d/. There is also an occasional upward glide at the end of a declarative sentence, as in the examples that follow.

Practice Exercises

1. Spanish phrases: *¿Como está Usted, señor? Muy bien, gracias. ¿Y Usted?*
/KO mo es TAH oo STED se NYAWR / MOOHee BYEN GRAH syahs / ee oo STED/

Translation: How are you, sir? Very well, thanks, and you?

Notes: If you want to learn a Spanish accent, learn a little of the language, so that you get the "feel" of how the muscles of the mouth are used. The /n/ at the end of *bien* is nasalized. Remember that final consonants are very soft. The word *gracias* (thanks) can have three syllables: /GRAH see ahs/ in an educated accent. In South American, Puerto Rican, and Cuban pronunciations the /s/ before /t/ in *está* (are) and *Usted* (you [formal]) is silent, as is the final /d/ in *Usted*: /KO mo e TAH oo TE/.

2. *You know what I mean.*
Castilian Spanish: /yooh NAW khwah dI MEEN/
Argentine: /yooh naw khwah dI MEEN/
Cuban, Puerto Rican: /zhooh naw hwahd I MEENG/
Mexican, Puerto Rican, Cuban: /jooh naw khwahd I MEENG/

Notes: The last two pronunciations represent a very heavy accent used by someone whose first language is Spanish. Depending on the particular pitch or intonation or musical pattern joined to it, these pronunciations are something of a cliché, used to great comic effect by the brilliant Spanish-American comedienne Charo. The forward and downward slashes here represent gliding upward and downward tones, stereotypical of Chicano English pronunciation.

Chicano English Pitch Pattern:

```
      know              /an.
                me-
  You       what I
```

3. *It's not very much, only forty-five pesos for that matter.*
General Spanish, Mexican, Puerto Rican, and South American: /ees no BE ree MAHSH / AWN lee FAWR dee FI PE sohs fawr da MA duh/

Notes: Notice all the dropped final consonants and the substitution of /b/ for /v/ in the word *very*. For a Chicano English accent, pronounce all the sounds as in General American, and make the /r/ very heavily retroflex, with the tongue curled well up and back; and lengthen the first syllables of *pesos* and *matter*.

Chicano English Pitch Pattern:

```
                                    matter.
                forty-
          much,        five        that
    not very     only      pesos
  It's                          for
```

4. *It's really freezing in here, because the landlord didn't turn on the heat.*
/ihs RIH lee FRIH sihng (alternatively, seen) ihn KHEER bih KAWS dee LAN lawr DIH den (alternatively, DIHN) TORN (alternatively, TAWRN) awn dee KHEE/

Notes: For a lighter accent, pronounce the retroflex /r/. For a heavier accent, give the /r/ one trill or flap. Notice the pronunciation of a light /kh/ substituting for initial /h/ sounds in *here* and *heat*. And notice the dropping of final /t/ in *heat*. Notice as well the use of the intermediate vowel /ih/.

Monologues

1. From Miguel Piñero's *Short Eyes* (1974), Act 2

This searing, award-winning prison drama by a man who had been to the hell he describes here, and who came out the other side to become a distinguished writer, concerns three black prisoners: Ice, Omar, and El Raheem; three Puerto Rican prisoners: Cupcakes, Paco, and Juan; two white prisoners: Longshoe, who is Irish, and Clark Davis; and their guards.

Paco /PAH ko/ is perfectly bilingual, and speaks colloquially. He also speaks some Spanish in the play, and has a heavier or lighter Hispanic accent in English, depending on the choice of the actor who plays the part. Final /z/ sounds, as in the word *is* or at the end of the first syllable of *wisdom*, should be pronounced as /s/.

> [CUPCAKES: Ain't nobody fucking me, Paco.]
>
> PACO. Maybe he's not yet, but he's setting you up. Giving you fatherly advice, my ass. He's just like El Raheem. He wants to fuck you too. Putting the wisdom in front of the knowledge. He's calling you a girl. That's what he means by that. And Omar playing exercises with you so that you can take showers together. Longshoe . . . giving you short-heist books. Everybody wants you, Cupcakes. Cupcakes, Ice gave you that name, didn't he? Wasn't that your woman's name in the street, Ice? . . . Nobody saying anything. Why? Cause I hit the truth. Pushed that little button . . . Everybody on the whole floor is trying to cop . . . but only Juan gets a share. Now he wants the white freak for himself, too.
>
> [JUAN: You're sick, man.]

PACO: Tu madre . . . tu madre, maricón . . . hijo de la gran puta . . . cabrón. [/tooh MAH dre / tooh MAH dre mah ree KON / EE kho de lah GRAHN POOH tah / kah BRON/ (Your mother . . . your mother, faggot . . . son of the big whore . . . bastard.)]

2. From Luis Valdez's *Bandido!*: *The American Melodrama of Tiburcio Vásquez, Notorious California Bandit* (1981), Act 1, Scene 3

Born in 1835 in Monterey, before Mexico had lost California to the United States during the Mexican War, Tiburcio Vásquez /tee BOOHR see o VAHS kes/, an educated man, a poet, and an avid reader, was blamed in 1854 for the death of a policeman on his property. He fled to escape lynching by a mob and became a notorious bandit, robbing stagecoaches and hiding in the mountains. Vásquez escaped from several prisons, but he was finally captured in 1873; he was executed two years later, in 1875.

Valdez's play with music, revived in 2009 in Carmel, California, fictionalizes the story and elaborates on history, giving it contemporary relevance and raising the issues of prejudice and nationalism. Tiburcio, whose first language was Spanish but who spoke excellent English, should have a light Mexican-Spanish accent, but that choice is up to the actor and the director.

Tiburcio has made Abdón Leiva his second in command because he is a dedicated man "of quality and distinction." Rita, Tiburcio's girlfriend, chides him for that choice, made because Abdón "obeys my orders implicitly," says Tiburcio. But Rita points out that he is burdened with "a high-class wife and blind father-in-law." Now he has failed to show up.

TIBURCIO: (*Ironic, smooth.*) Quality is a rare commodity, Rita. This blind man and his family used to own half of northern California. Yes, we will wait for Leiva. Now to our melodrama. I have the guns. Let me see your get-ups. And I want to see some tough, mean looking hombres. (MORENO *steps up for inspection, followed by the others.*) Cousin, good to have you with us. [. . .] You're a bandido now. Look sloppy and more desperate. (MORENO *dirties his suit*.) Good, you get the Henry rifle. Gonzales, you look like a natural born greaser.

[GONZALES: Gracias, jefe . . . I think. [/GRAH syahs KHE fe/ (Thanks, boss)]]

TIBURCIO: We've ridden together before. You're more experienced than the others. You get the shotgun. But control yourself, hombre. You'd scare your own mother. Chávez, as the new recruit, welcome. But do me a favor. Pull that sombrero down a little . . . No, that's too much . . . That's better. Good! That's it. You get a dragoon revolver.

3. From José Rivera's *Cloud Tectonics* (1996)

Anibal de la Luna /ah nee BAHL de lah LOOH nah/ meets the pregnant Celestina del Sol /se les TEE nah del SOL/ at a bus stop during a torrential rainstorm. She is desperate and having labor pains. Celestina has nowhere to go, and Anibal kindly takes her to his house.

Celestina's accent is clearly very light, and she is obviously bilingual. Perhaps she would have only a hard /r/ and an /s/ substituted for a final /z/ sound to indicate her linguistic background. The name of her lover should be pronounced perfectly: /ro DREE go KROOHS/.

CELESTINA: I think about sex all the time, though I've only had one lover in my life, only one time, Rodrigo Cruz. And I almost had two! That despicable trucker who kept touching my knees. But I ran away from him. I took my chances in the rain. But even he couldn't stop my endless daydreaming and nightdreaming about sex: about Rodrigo's wrinkled back, my legs wrapped around his face . . . this obsession of mine . . . this tidal wave that started sometime when I was younger, when I lived in that one room. When Papi bought me a bicycle to give me something else to think about besides my body, and one glorious day I was allowed to ride around and around the house, because my Papi wanted me to count numbers, count numbers, over and over; he said it would teach me about the nature of "time," and I tried and tried, I really did, but I didn't learn anything, I was just so grateful to be outside my little room for once!

4. From Nilo Cruz's *Hortensia and the Museum of Dreams* (2001), "Fresh Water from the River Ariguanabo" /ah REE gwah NAH bo/

This play, by renowned Cuban-American playwright Nilo Cruz, is set during "the Pope's visit, January 21–25, 1998." Amparo de las Rosas lives in a small apartment with her husband in impoverished Havana, and she doesn't know where her next mouthful will come from. But she thinks she has experienced a miracle because of the pope's visit.

The Spanish names should be perfectly pronounced: Amparo de las Rosas /ahm PAH raw de las RAW sahs/, Céspedes /SES pe des/, Isidro /ee SEE draw/—the /aw/ sounds are quite short. The soft /d/ sounds are close to /th/. Since Amparo is presumably speaking Spanish, there need not be any accent other than the actor's own, or one she chooses. As she plays multiple parts, however, a slight Spanish intonation pattern and perhaps the substitution of /s/ for /z/ may be used for this character, in the words *residing, miserable, husband, birds, windows,* and *was.*

AMPARO (*Wears rollers in her hair*): My name is Amparo de las Rosas. I am a seamstress residing at Céspedes Street. On the seventh of May the only thing my husband and I had to eat was a miserable potato that I fried in a pan with some rancid lard. That night my husband, Isidro, and I kneeled down in front of the altar and prayed for food. The next morning a flock of birds flew into the house, and I told Isidro to close all the windows to catch some of those God-sent creatures. The house and the patio were full of parrots, turkeys, doves, even birds I'd never seen.

That was our miracle because Isidro and I had food for a month. Later that day we heard on the news that an old tree had fallen on a bird cage at the zoo and hundreds of birds had escaped. But those birds that flew into our house weren't from the zoo. That was our miracle.

7

Some Urban Accents:
New Orleans, Chicago, Boston, New York

Every city has a variety of pronunciation models, often different from those of the surrounding countryside. More urban accents are discussed elsewhere in this book: Baltimore, Maryland, and Detroit, Michigan, in chapter 2; and Charleston, South Carolina, in chapter 3.

Teach Yourself New Orleans Accents

New Orleans has an accent often said to resemble those of Hoboken, New Jersey, or Brooklyn, New York. The pronunciations of streets and places with French names, despite the city's French background, bear little relationship to the original language, beginning with the name of the city itself: New Orleans—/nyooh AWR lee uhnz/ in General American—is pronounced variously by its inhabitants as /nyooh AW luhnz/, /NOO aw LEENZ/, /nyooh aw LEENZ/, /NAW luhnz/, or /NYAW luhnz/. In French, *Orléans* is pronounced /awr lé AWN/, with the final /n/ nasalized. *Bourbon* (/boor BON/, with the /n/ nasalized, in French) is pronounced /BOR (alternatively, BOY, or BOYR) buhn/ in New Orleans, Chartres (French: /SHAHR truh/) is /CHAHR tuhrz/, and Lake Pontchartrain (French: /pawn shahr TREN/, with the /e/ lengthened and the two /n/ sounds nasalized) is pronounced /PAHN shuh TRAYN/. The name *Burgundy* is stressed on the second syllable: /buh GUN dee/.

The city has loomed large in American literature and in the American imagination. Kate Chopin's late-nineteenth-century stories, among them *The Awakening* (1899), and Anne Rice's *The Vampire Chronicles*, beginning with *Interview with the Vampire* (1976), are set in New Orleans. John Grisham set *The Pelican Brief* and *The Client* there; they were filmed in 1993 and 1994, respectively. New Orleans is known as "The Big Easy," which is also the title of the 1986 film starring Dennis Quaid. *Sonny* (2002), starring James Franco, also takes place in New Orleans. Although Tennessee Williams's *A Streetcar Named Desire* unfolds in New Orleans, in the famous 1951 film no attempt is made to do the accent; this hardly matters given the brilliant performances. Another Williams play, *Vieux Carré* /VYOO ka RÉ/ (1977), is also set in New Orleans.

Here are the elements of the New Orleans accents:

1. **Positioning, placement, and use of the muscles of the mouth during speech:** The mouth is fairly open and loose jawed. The tongue wants to rest at the bottom of the mouth.

2. **The sounds of /r/:** The accent is inconsistent: it is largely non-rhotic, so post-vocalic (after a vowel) /r/ is not pronounced; *river* is heard as /RIH vuh/. But there is an occasional rhotic pronunciation: *Where you at?* /wer YAT/. And some speakers' accents are entirely rhotic.

3. **Vowels and diphthongs:** There are few shifts from General American.
   a. **The shift from /ah/ to /aw/:** The /ah/ in *father* shifts to /aw/: /FAW thuh/, *department* /dih PAWT mihnt/.
   b. **Verb participles ending in "-ed":** Words ending in "-ed," such as *married*, shift the ending to /ihd/: /MA rihd/.
   c. **The shifts from /ih/ to /e/ and from /e/ to /ih/:** As usual in other Southern accents, this shift is also heard in New Orleans: *thing* /TENG (alternatively, THENG)/, *pen* /PIHN (alternatively, PEEuhn)/.

    d. **The shift from /I/ to /ah/:** In working-class New Orleans accents the /I/ diphthong shifts to the vowel /ah/, as in the other Southern accents, with /ee/, the second half of the diphthong, dropped: *time* /TAHM/. This is not always the case, and one sometimes hears the General American diphthong /I/.

    e. **Words ending in "-ow":** Words ending in "-ow," such as *fellow* or *yellow*, shift the diphthong in the last syllable to the schwa: /FE luh/, /YE luh/.

    f. **The shift of /o/ to /oy/:** The sound of the vowel in *work* and *first* sometimes shifts to /oy/ or, more accurately, to the diphthong /Uee/: /WUeek/, /FUeest/. The famous chef Paul Prudhomme pronounces *dessert* as /dih ZOYRT/, with the /r/ lightly pronounced.

    g. **The shift of /oy/ to /aw/:** The diphthong /oy/, whether in *boy*, *boil*, or *oil*, shifts to /aw/: /BAW/, /BAWL/, /AWL/.

    h. **The sound of /u/:** The sound of /u/ in such words as *but* and *above* often, but not always, shifts to /o/: /BOT/, /uh BOV/.

    i. **Diphthongization:** Elongated diphthongized vowels and sometimes triphthongs are often heard, as in the following examples: *The music stops here* /duh MYOOH zihk stop SYEEuh/, *court* /KAWwuht/.

    j. **Nasalization:** In a Cajun accent, there is often heavy nasalization of vowels: *Alabama* /A luh MBA muh/.

4. **Other consonants:** Consonants are the same as in General American, with the following exceptions:

    a. **Consonant cluster reduction:** The final consonant in a cluster is dropped; so, for instance, the /t/ at end of /st/ is not pronounced: *last* /LAS/. The /r/ is sometimes dropped in the word *pretty*, pronounced /POO dee/, with tapped /d/.

    b. **Final /g/-dropping:** The /g/ in "-ing" endings is often, but not always, dropped.

c. **Dropping of /l/:** Particularly in working-class accents, /l/ in the middle of a word is dropped: *help* /HEP/, *jewelry* /JOOH ree/, *celery* /SE ree/.

d. **The sound of /ch/:** In a Cajun accent, the final /ch/ is often heard as /j/. The word *church* is pronounced /CHOJ/, for example.

e. **The tapped /d/:** A tapped /d/ replaces the /z/ sound in words like *business* and *isn't*: /BIHD nihs/, /IHD n/, with /t/ dropped.

f. **The sounds of /th / th/:** Voiced /th/ in *this*, *them*, *these*, and *those* is often pronounced like /d/: *There you go* /DE yuh GOH/. Voiceless /th/ is often /t/: *through* /TROOH/, *think* /TIHNK/. Sometimes, initial /th/ is dropped: *in the* /IH nuh/. Among educated speakers, these sounds are correctly pronounced.

Intonation and Stress: The Music and Rhythm of the Accents

New Orleans accents have a music that comes partly from Cajun French and partly from the Southern drawl. There is sometimes a rising tone at the end of a declarative sentence when the speaker wishes to emphasize a point. But, generally, the intonation is flat and follows General American patterns.

Practice Exercises

1. *She was married in a yellow gown and I enjoyed the crawfish boil we had for a wedding feast with celery and dips and other goodies and a gorgeous wedding cake.*

/shee wuz MA rihd ihn uh YE luh GOWN en ah ihn JAWD duh KRAW fihsh BAWL wee had faw ruh WE dihn FEEST wihd SE ree an DIHPS an U thuh GOO dihz an uh GAW jihs WE dihn KAYK/

2. Practice for the shift from /o/ to /oy/: *heard, first, work, learn, bird, word*; /HOYD/, /FOYST/, /WOYK/, /LOYN/, /BOYD/, /WOYD/.

Note: Sometimes a lightly pronounced /r/ is heard: /HOYRD/, etc.

3. *Well, that's pretty good. They was real good years when he was working down there by Lake Pontchartrain.*
/wel das POO dee GOOD / day wuz RIHL good YEEZ wen hee wuz WOY kihn down de bah LAYK PAHN shuh TRAYN/

Note: The vowels in *years* and *there* are very long.

4. *I expect she'll wear her fine jewelry and be carried in on the shoulders of her admirers from the Ninth Ward during Mardi Gras. Maybe they'll go to Gallatoire's or the Commander's Palace.*
/ah SPEK shihl WEuh huh fahn JOOH ree an bee KA rih dihn awn duh SHOH duhz uhv huh rad MAH ruhz fm duh NINT WAWD DOO rihn MAW dee GRAH / MAY bih dayl GOH duh GA lah twahz aw duh kuh MAN duhz PA lihs/

Note: The /d/ sounds in the syllables /dihn/, /dee/, /dayl/, and /duh/ are tapped.

A Monologue and a Scene for Two
1. From Tennessee Williams's *A Streetcar Named Desire* (1947), Scene 3, "The Poker Night"
While his wife, Stella, and her sister, Blanche, have gone out, soon to return, Stanley Kowalski plays poker with his buddies Steve, Mitch, and Pablo.

> STEVE [. . .]: Seven card stud. (*Telling his joke as he deals*) This ole farmer is out in back of his house sittin' down th'owing corn to the chickens when all at once he hears a loud cackle and this young hen comes lickety split around the side of the house with the rooster right behind her and gaining on her fast.
> [STANLEY (*Impatient with the story*): Deal!]
> STEVE: But when the rooster catches sight of the farmer th'owing the corn he puts on the brakes and lets the hen get away and starts

pecking corn. And the old farmer says, "Lord God, I hope I never gits *that* hongry!"

2. From Tennessee Williams's *Vieux Carré* /VYOO ka RÉ/ (1977), Part 1, Scene 4

The title of this autobiographical play means "Old Square," from the play's setting in the New Orleans French Quarter. During the Great Depression of the 1930s, Mrs. Wire, in the dilapidated boarding house she runs, is "preparing a big pot of gumbo." She is talking with one of her boarders, an impoverished writer, who is dressed "in all that remains of his wardrobe: riding boots and britches, a faded red flannel shirt."

The WPA was the Roosevelt administration's Works Projects Administration, which employed thousands in various jobs.

MRS. WIRE: Who, who?—Aw, you dressed up like a jockey in a donkey race!

WRITER: —My, uh, clothes are at the cleaners.

MRS. WIRE: Do they clean clothes at the pawnshop, yeah, I reckon they do clean clothes not redeemed. Oh. Don't go upstairs. Your room is forfeited, too.

WRITER: . . . You mean I'm . . . ?

MRS. WIRE: A loser, boy. Possibly you could git a cot at the Salvation Army.

WRITER (*averting his eyes*): May I sit down a moment?

MRS. WIRE: Why, for what?

WRITER: Eviction presents . . . a problem.

MRS. WIRE: I thought you was gittin' on the WPA Writers' Project? That's what you tole me when I inquired about your prospects for employment, you said, "Oh, I've applied for work on the WPA for writers."

WRITER: I couldn't prove that my father was destitute, and the fact he contributes nothing to my support seemed—immaterial to them.

MRS. WIRE: Why're you shifty-eyed? I never seen a more shifty-eyed boy.

WRITER: I, uh, have had a little eye trouble, lately.

Teach Yourself Chicago Accents

For authentic Chicago accents, which have variations on the North Side and South Side, listen to Joe Mantegna in *The Godfather Part III* (1989), *Glengarry Glen Ross* (1992), and the television series *Criminal Minds* (2005–); and to Bill Murray, born and raised in the Chicago suburb of Winnetka, in *What About Bob?* (1991) and *Groundhog Day* (1993). And listen to the elegant diction of Illinois-born William Holden in *Stalag 17* (1953), *Sunset Boulevard* (1950), and *The Counterfeit Traitor* (1962). The comedian Jack Benny, born in Chicago, retained more than a touch of his native accent. See him in DVDs of his TV series *The Jack Benny Program* (1950–1965) and the theatrical films *To Be or Not to Be* (1942) and *The Horn Blows at Midnight* (1945).

1. **Positioning, placement, and use of the muscles of the mouth during speech:** The general position of the muscles during speech feels tight and the lips are drawn out to the sides a bit. The accents "feel" as though they are pronounced in the middle of the mouth. The back of the tongue is tensed slightly during speech.

2. **The sound of /r/:** The accent is rhotic, so post-vocalic (after a vowel) /r/ is pronounced. The hard /r/ is pronounced with the back of the tongue tensed.

3. **Vowels and diphthongs:**
   a. **The schwa before /r/:** The schwa is used in words like *there*, when unstressed, and *sure* /SHUHR/, even when stressed: *There sure is* /thuhr SHUHR ihz/.
   b. **The sound of /a/:** The sound of /a/ in *cat* and *that* is very flat and closed, and is sometimes diphthongized to /Auh/.

    c. **The shift from /aw/ to /ah/:** As in other Midwestern accents, such words as *all*, *talk*, and *walk*, pronounced with a long /aw/ in General American, are pronounced with /ah/: /AHL/, /TAHK/, /WAHK/.

  4. **Other consonants:** Consonants are hard and well articulated. Chicago accents are generally very clear.

Intonation and Stress: The Music and Rhythm of the Accents

The intonation patterns for Chicago are the same as for General American, with a drop in pitch at the end of declarative sentences, and a rise at the end of questions.

Practice Exercises

1. *I'm sure there's nothing at all that can't be made that much simpler with hard work.*
/ahm SHUHR thuhrz NU *thing* e DAHL thet KANT bee MAYD thet much SIHM pluhr wih*th* HAHRD WORK/

Notes: The /d/ in /DAHL/ is tapped. The /a/ in /KANT/ is very flat. Final /t/ in /thet/ is very light.

2. *I've been there quite a few times. I heard of a guy that went down there and lost his shirt.*
/Iv BEN THER kwI dah fyooh TIMZ / I HOR duhv uh GI duht went DOWN uhr auhn LOST ihz SHORT/

Note: The /d/ sounds in the syllables /dah/, /duhv/, and /duht/ are tapped.

3. *Be serious for a moment. That's just an impossible situation.*
/bee SIHuh ree uhs fuhr uh MOH muhnt / THAuhTS just auhn ihm PAH sih buhl sih chooh AY shuhn/

4. *"Oh, brother," I said, "that's really something else!" "Oh, really? What else is*
it?" he said. He was always a real wiseguy.
/oh BRU thuhr I sed THAuhTS RIH lee SUM thihng (alternatively, SUM?
m) ELS / oh RIH lee WAH dels ihz it hee sed / hee wuhz AHL weez uh
REEuhL WIZ GI/

Note: The /d/ in the syllable /dels/ is tapped.

Monologues

1. From David Mamet's One-Act Comedy *Sexual Perversity in Chicago* (1974)

Many of David Mamet's plays are set in Chicago, his home city.

Joan is a nursery school teacher who goes to singles bars. Here she is
"lecturing two toddlers at the school" about what they have been up to.
This excerpt shows the stereotypical discomfort adults have on the subject
of childhood sexuality, decades after Freud analyzed the stages of human
psycho-sexual development.

JOAN: What are you doing? Where are you going? What are you
doing? You stay right there. Now. What were the two of you doing?
I'm just asking a simple question. There's nothing to be ashamed
of. (*Pause.*) I can wait. (*Pause.*) Were you playing "Doctor"? (*Pause.*)
"Doctor." Don't play dumb with me, just answer the question. (You
know, that attitude is going to get you in a lot of trouble someday.)
Were you playing with each other's genitals? Each other's . . . "pee-
pees"?—whatever you call them at home, that's what I'm asking.
(And don't play dumb, because I saw what you were doing, so just
own up to it.) (*Pause.*) Alright . . . no. No, stop that, there's no
reason for tears . . . it's perfectly . . . natural. But . . . there's a time
and a place for everything. Now . . . no, it's alright. Come on. Come
on, we're all going to the other room, and we're going to wash our
hands. And then Miss Webber is going to call our parents.

2. From David Mamet's *Glengarry Glen Ross* (1982), Act 1, Scene 2
This Pulitzer Prize–winning play about the development of the housing
estate of Glengarry Glen Ross deals with the cynicism, hopes, struggles,
and aspirations of seven realtors.

Moss, a man in his fifties, is talking to a younger colleague, Aaronow.
Moss displays his appalling anti-Indian bigotry. Mamet understands the
nature of prejudice and its relation to sexual insecurity very well, and even
has Moss talk in terms of Indians' sexuality. Moss projects his own inner
demons, and it is he who is supercilious, and in denial about his own feel-
ings of being sexually like "a dead *cat*." By "one," Moss means a person to
whom they won't be able to sell anything.

> MOSS: You had one you'd know it. *Patel.* They keep coming up. I
> don't know. They like to talk to salesmen. (*pause*) They're *lonely*,
> something. (*pause*) They like to feel *superior*, I don't know. Never
> bought a fucking thing. You're sitting down. "The Rio Rancho
> *this*, the blah, blah, blah," "The Mountain View—" "Oh yes. My
> brother told me that . . ." They got a grapevine. Fuckin' Indians,
> George. Not my cup of tea. Speaking of which I want to tell you
> something. (*pause*) I never got a cup of tea with them. You see
> them in the restaurants. A supercilious race. What is this *look* on
> their face all the time? I don't know. (*pause*) I don't know. Their
> broads all looked like they just got fucked with a dead *cat*, I don't
> know. (*pause*) I don't know. I don't like it. Christ . . .

Teach Yourself Boston Accents

There are several Boston and Massachusetts accents. Listen, for example, to
Bette Davis, who was from Lowell, Massachusetts. The individual, distinctive accent of the Kennedy family, which can be heard in many recordings
and documentary films, is very broad, and is similar to the Boston Back

Bay accents described below. Among other things, the Kennedys tend to lengthen stressed vowels and diphthongs slightly.

The Departed (2006) and *Southie* (1998) take place in Boston, and feature authentic accents. *Good Will Hunting* (1997), which takes place at Harvard, stars Boston-born Matt Damon; his friend Ben Affleck, born in Berkeley, California, but raised in Cambridge; and Ben's brother, Casey. The three actors usually speak with a General American accent, but they can do the Boston accent perfectly. And listen to news commentator Mark Shields, from Weymouth, near Boston, for an authentic accent.

1. **Positioning, placement, and use of the muscles of the mouth during speech:** The general position of the muscles during speech feels slightly tight and the lips are tensed at the corners a bit. The accents "feel" as though they are pronounced in the middle of the mouth. The back of the tongue is tensed slightly during speech.

2. **The sounds of /r/:** Generally, Boston accents were strongly non-rhotic in the past, with a silent post-vocalic (after a vowel) /r/, but that is not always the case now. A very lightly pronounced post-vocalic /r/ is often heard, and final vowels followed by /r/ are usually r-influenced.

3. **Vowels and diphthongs:**

   a. **The sounds of /a/ and /ah/:** In an old-fashioned accent, Bostonians say *answer*, *ask*, *aunt*, *bath*, *can't*, *dance*, and *last* with the /ah/ in *father*; but the younger generations pronounce those words with /a/. In Boston, *Boston* is /BAH stuhn/, whereas to a New Yorker the city is /BAW stihn/. In the Back Bay area, the /ah/ in *park* is pronounced like the /a/ in *that*: /PAK/. Elsewhere in the city, *park* is pronounced as in General American, with the vowel /ah/: /PAHK (alternatively, PAHRK)/.

   b. **The schwa:** Sometimes, a schwa is inserted after /e/ and before an /r/ in such words as *caring* and *daring*: /KEuh rihng/, /DEuh rihng/. In unstressed syllables, the schwa is used somewhat as it is in British RP, so *business*, for example, is pronounced /BIHZ nuhs/. Some Bostonians say *going to* as /GUH nuh/ or sometimes as /GU nuh/ (where the /u/ is the sound in *but*). For words ending in /aw/ followed by /r/, such as *door* and *floor*, a schwa is often heard, replacing the /r/ and making the word into two syllables: /DOH uh/, /FLOH uh/.

   c. **The shift of /aw/ to /ah/ or /o/:** The vowel /aw/ shifts to the /ah/ in *father*, much as in the Midwest, but the sound is more closed. In an upper-class accent, /aw/ shifts to /o/ as in *hot* or *not*.

   d. **The sound of /o/:** The vowel /o/ in *hot*, *not*, and *got* is short, and tends toward /aw/, much as in Standard British English.

   e. **The sound of /ooh/:** The semi-vowel /y/ is not usually inserted between a consonant and /ooh/ in lower-class Boston speech, so *news* and *duke* are pronounced /NOOHZ/ and /DOOHK/. In upper-class Boston Brahmin speech, /y/ is often inserted: /NYOOHZ/, /DYOOHK/.

4. **Other consonants:** Consonants are distinctly articulated, and do not vary from General American.

Intonation and Stress: The Music and Rhythm of the Accents

The intonation patterns for Boston are the same as for General American, with a drop in pitch at the end of declarative sentences, and a rise at the end of questions.

Practice Exercises

1. *Park your car in Harvard Yard.*
Back Bay: /PAK yuh KA rihn HA vuhd YAD/
Upper-class Boston Brahmin: /PAHK yuh KAH rihn HAH vuhd YAHD/

Notes: The vowels in the Brahmin accent are r-influenced. As in all non-rhotic accents, there is a "linking /r/," so *car in* is pronounced /KAH rihn/.

The Back Bay pronunciation of this well-known sentence has become something of a cliché, so be very careful not to exaggerate the flat /a/ substitution for /ah/, and to pronounce the r-influenced vowel sounds.

2. *The law is not very formal and strict in that regard.*
Back Bay: /thuh LA ruhz naht VE ree FAH muhl an STRIHKT ihn that ree GAD/
Upper-class Boston Brahmin: /thuh LO rihz not VE ree FO muhl an STRIHKT ihn that ruh GAHD/

Notes: Do not exaggerate the shift of /aw/ to /ah/ in such words as *formal*: The trick is to think /aw/ but say /ah/. In the Brahmin pronunciation, *law* could be pronounced without the linking /r/: /LO ihz/.

3. *The weather has cleared up nicely, so we can go outdoors again, and the ice on the Charles River is starting to melt.*
Back Bay: /thuh WE thuh haz KLEE dup NIS lee soh wee kin goh OWT DAWZ uh GEN and thee IS awn thuh CHALZ RIH vuh ihz (alternatively, rihz) STA ding tuh MELT/
Upper-class Boston Brahmin: /thuh WE thuh haz KLEEuh dup NIS lee soh wee kuhn GOH owt DOHuhZ uh GEN and thee IS ahn thuh CHAHLZ RIH vuh rihz STAH ding tuh MELT/

Notes: The /d/ sounds in the syllables /dup/ and /ding/ are tapped. Notice that the sounds of "a" in *Charles* and *starting* vary: in the Brahmin accent they are /ah/; in the Back Bay, /a/; the /r/ is dropped in both accents.

4. *There are certain things to be done at certain times, as a last resort, provided that is necessary, as far as what you are describing.*
General Boston: /thuh rah SO ?n thihngz tuh bee dun at SO ?n tImz az uh LAHST rih ZAWT (alternatively, ZAW?) pruh VI dihd tha dihz NE suh SE ree ez FAH ruhz waht yaw (alternatively, yooh ah) dih SKRI bihng/

Notes: Notice the glottal stops in the word *certain*, the tapped /t/ or glottal stop (speaker's choice) in *resort*, the tapped first /d/ in the syllables /dihd/ and /dihz/, and the lengthened /ah/ sounds in the words *last* and *far*. You also have a choice of pronunciations for *you are*. If the second /r/ in *resort* is pronounced, it is very light.

Monologues

1. From Tina Howe's *Painting Churches* (1983)

Mags Church, a portrait painter and the daughter of the distinguished poet Gardner Church, has come from New York to the Church family's Boston town house to paint her father's portrait. Gardner is growing senile, and his wife, Fanny, Mags's mother, tries to stave off despair. Mags talks to her mother as she is preparing the room and her easel.

> MAGS: Remember how you behaved at my first group show in Soho? . . . Oh, come on, you remember. It was a real circus! Think back . . . It was about six years ago . . . Daddy had just been awarded some presidential medal of achievement and you insisted he wear it around his neck on a bright red ribbon, and you wore this . . . *huge* feathered hat to match! I'll never forget it! It was the size of a giant pizza with twenty-inch red turkey feathers shooting straight up into the air . . . Oh, come on, you remember, don't you . . . ?

2. From Deborah Eisenberg's *Pastorale* (1982)

In a New England farmhouse, John, in his twenties, is visiting Rachel, a guest of Melanie and Steve, who have rented the house. We may assume from what they tell us about their lives that they are from Boston. While John talks to Melanie, he runs "his hand up her leg." You might try this excerpt with a Back Bay accent.

> JOHN: [. . .] I remember once I was at this concert, and there was this chick sitting in the seat next to me. And she was, like, older,

but she was pretty good looking, and she looked really, really sad. Well, I remember I had just washed my hair, which was pretty long then, and it was all sort of electric. And I realized it was sort of brushing against this woman when I'd turn around, and I wondered if it was annoying her. But then I noticed she was beginning to lean a bit towards me when I'd turn, and also I saw that she was sort of looking at my hands. I mean, I really wasn't sure, so I rolled up my sleeves, really slowly. Like this . . . And I sort of stretched my arms out on the arm rests. Well she was definitely looking at my arms. No question about it. So, I was staring at the stage like I was really absorbed in the concert, and I leaned my head just a little bit towards her.

Teach Yourself New York City Accents

There are several New York City accents: Manhattan, Bronx, Brooklyn, and Queens. The old-fashioned accents are all non-rhotic and at the same time r-influenced. New York City accents have been influenced by immigrant communities, notably Irish, Italian, Eastern European Jewish, and Hispanic, as well as by AAVE: "Uh-uh" for *no* and "uh-huh" and "mm-hm" for *yes*, universally heard in New York City, are originally African-American expressions, to take but three examples.

The old-fashioned, elegant upper-class New York accent used by President Franklin D. Roosevelt is practically gone. And the original middle- and working-class non-rhotic New York accents are undergoing alteration, but those discussed here are certainly useful for plays set in the past, like those of Clifford Odets, Arthur Miller, or Neil Simon. (See the films of Simon's plays, such as *Biloxi Blues* [1988], starring Matthew Broderick and Christopher Walken—from Manhattan and Queens, respectively—for some good examples of the accents.) Most educated New Yorkers have rhotic accents, with the /r/ very lightly pronounced. The working-class accents tend to be more broadly non-rhotic, though this is a vast stereotype. Queens and Long Island accents have a reputation for being rather nasal, like the speech of Fran Drescher, from Flushing, Queens, in her television series *The Nanny* (1993–1999), although this is by no means always the case.

See Newark-born Joe Pesci as the slumlord in *The Super* (1991), and as the lawyer in the riotously funny *My Cousin Vinny* (1992), along with the Academy Award–winning Marisa Tomei, for great New York City–area accents. And don't miss *Married to the Mob* (1988), starring Queens-born Mercedes Ruehl, Alec Baldwin (from Long Island), and Dean Stockwell, who does a perfect New York accent although he is from Hollywood. Among other actors with a variety of native New York City accents are Burt Lancaster; James Cagney; Jackie Gleason, whose celebrated TV series *The Honeymooners* (1955–1956) is set in Brooklyn; Sammy Davis, Jr., in *Ocean's 11* (1960), etc.; Woody Allen; Whoopi Goldberg; Dom DeLuise; George Burns; Rosie O'Donnell from Long Island; Harvey Fierstein—see *Torch Song Trilogy* (1988), based on his Broadway play; Barbra Streisand—see *Funny Girl* (1968) and *The Way We Were* (1973), both set in New York; Judd Hirsch; Paul Sorvino; Jerry Stiller, Anne Meara, and their son, Ben Stiller; Carl Reiner and his son Rob Reiner; Groucho Marx; and Mel Brooks, who was married to Anne Bancroft, a native of the Bronx. Bancroft could use her New York City accent when her roles demanded it, as in *Garbo Talks* (1984) and *84 Charing Cross Road* (1987). See George Burns and his fellow New Yorker Walter Matthau in Neil Simon's *The Sunshine Boys* (1975), set in New York City, like so many of his comedies. More New York actors to listen to include Billy Crystal, Danny Aiello, Armand Assante, Luther Adler, Lee J. Cobb, Long Island–born Rodney Dangerfield, Bronx-born James Caan, Robert De Niro, Al Pacino, Richard Dreyfuss, and Hector Elizondo.

For examples of New York Hispanic-American accents, listen to the recording of the 2008 Broadway musical *In the Heights* (see chapter 6 for more information on Hispanic accents) by Lin-Manuel Miranda, who also stars, and Quiara Alegría Hudes. The story takes place in the Dominican-American community in Washington Heights.

Here are the hallmarks of the New York City accents:

1. **Positioning, placement, and use of the muscles of the mouth during speech:** The general position of the muscles during speech feels loose and the lips are protruded just a bit. The accents "feel" as though they are pronounced in the middle of the mouth. The tongue is relaxed during speech.

2. **The sounds of /r/:** Some New York City accents are non-rhotic, so post-vocalic (after a vowel) /r/ is not pronounced. But many people speak with a rhotic accent, and in educated New York speech and general Manhattan speech, /r/ is very lightly pronounced. Even in non-rhotic New York City accents post-vocalic /r/ is sometimes pronounced: *My father told me the other day* /mI FAH (alternatively, FAW) thuhr TOHLD mee thee U thuh day/. And there is an intrusive /r/ in such phrases as *the idea is* and *law and order*: /thee I DEE rihz/, /LAW ran AW duh/, pronounced with a tapped /d/. The word *idea* is sometimes pronounced /I DEER/, with an intrusive /r/, even when there is no occasion for a linking /r/. There is also a linking /r/: *there is* /the RIHZ/.

3. **Vowels and diphthongs:**
   a. **The use of /ih/ in unstressed syllables:** Instead of a schwa in unstressed syllables, an /ih/ is often heard: *island* is /I lihnd/, *forward* is /FAW wihd/.
   b. **The shift from /ah/ to /aw/:** The /ah/ in *father* is often pronounced with the /aw/ in *law*: /FAW thuh/; *park* is /PAWK/. By no means universal, this shift is heard in the speech of older native New Yorkers and Long Islanders.
   c. **The sound of /a/:** For a typical lower-class very flat pronunciation of this vowel, the lips are closed and narrowed to either side, as in the famous phrase *I can't stand it* /I kan? STAN di?/, with or without a glottal stop.

d. **The sound of /aw/:** The /aw/ in *coffee, law, New York, off, offer, talk,* and *walk* is a long sound, pronounced with the mouth narrowly open and the lips slightly protruded: /KAW fee/, /LAW/, /NOOH YAWK/, /AWF/, /AW fuh/, /TAWK/, /WAWK/.

e. **The shift of /I/ or /o/ to /oy/:** The diphthong /I/ shifts in old-fashioned New York accents to /oy/, especially in the speech of uneducated New Yorkers. The words *like* and *night* are pronounced /LOYK/ and /NOYT/, but the /oy/ is pronounced with a short /UHee/ instead of a long /AWee/. Sometimes, an /r/ is heard in such words as *first* and *work* /FUHeeRST (alternatively, FOYST)/, /WUHeeRK (alternatively, WOYK)/, a trait associated with a New York Jewish accent. On the other hand, *I'm* is usually pronounced /ahm/ when not stressed. *I'm here* is heard variously as /ahm HEEuh/ or /oym HEEuh/—especially in an old-time New York Jewish accent; /ahm HEER/, which is general New York City and New York Irish as well as New York Hispanic-American; or /ahm HEE/, with perhaps a slight schwa after /HEE/, particularly in a New York Italian accent. Now rarely heard is the tendency, usually associated with old-time Brooklyn accents, to pronounce /o/ as /oy/ in such words as *first* and *work*; *Thirty-Third Street* was once heard as /TOY dee TOYD STREET/, with a long /AWee/ sound.

f. **The shift from /o/ to /ah/:** Ubiquitous in all New York City accents, the short /o/ in *bottle, got, not, on,* and *sorry* is pronounced with the /ah/ in *father*: /BAH ?l/ or /BAH tuhl/, /GAHT (alternatively, GAH?)/, /NAHT (alternatively, NAH?)/, /AHN/, /SAH ree/.

g. **The sound of /ooh/:** The vowel /ooh/ in the words *news* and *duke* is almost never pronounced /yooh/ in lower-class New York speech, where these words are pronounced /NOOHZ/ and /DOOHK/. But educated New Yorkers often say /NYOOHZ/ and /DYOOHK/.

4. **Other consonants:** Consonants in educated speech are the same as for General American, fairly light, but there are several phenomena to bear in mind:

   a. **Dentalization of /d/ and /t/:** The consonants /t/ and /d/ at the end of a word are often heavily aspirated, especially in Brooklyn, and there is an occasional tendency (associated most often with Brooklyn, Queens, and Long Island, and with New York Jewish accents) to dentalize /t/ and /d/, heard as /ts/ and /dz/ at the beginning of words. Also, /tr/ in some lower-class accents shifts to /chr/, so *try* is pronounced /CHRI/ or /CHROY/. Similarly, /dr/ shifts to /jr/, so *dry* is pronounced /JRI/ or /JROY/. A tapped /d/ is often heard as a substitute for /t/, as in the following examples of *Try to do it*: Queens, /TSROY tsuh (alternatively, duh, with a tapped /d/) dzooh it (alternatively, IHTS, or IH?)/; Brooklyn, /TROY de dooh it (alternatively, IH?)/. Note that the final /t/ is strongly aspirated, or, alternatively, dentalized.

   b. **The added /g/:** In a stereotypical Long Island accent (known also for its flat vowels: /ah/ shifts to /aw/, as in *father* /FAW thuh/; /a/ is very flat), a final /g/ is added to the /ng/ in such words as *long* and *sing*: /LAWNGG/, /SHINGG/, *Long Island* /LAWNGG I lihnd/. This is also heard in the speech of some New York Jewish residents, perhaps due to the influence of Yiddish, where such sounds are a part of the language. On the other hand, these were apparently the usual Elizabethan pronunciations.

   c. **Consonant cluster reduction and dropped consonants:** The final /g/ in "-ing" endings is typically dropped, especially in working-class accents. Sometimes certain initial and/or final consonants are dropped by educated and uneducated New Yorkers. The words *going to* are /GAW nuh/, or /UH nuh/, with the initial and final /g/ and the /t/ in *to* dropped. *I'm going to go now* becomes /AHM uh nuh GOH now/. Initial /th/ is often dropped: *Is that so?* is heard as /ih ZAT SOH/, with the /z/ in *is* linked to the /a/ in *that*. *That's right* is pronounced /ats RIT/, or /ATS rIt/, or even /AS rI?/.

d. **The sounds of /l/ and /l/-dropping:** The pronunciation of /l/ is usually as it is in General American. In the speech of some Hispanic-American New Yorkers, a Spanish /l/ is sometimes heard; see p. 77. A general New York City (and, especially, Brooklyn) feature is the occasional dropping of /l/, even in the speech of educated New Yorkers, in certain words: *almost* and *always* are universally pronounced /OH MOHST/ and /OH wayz/ or /OH weez/, especially when the word is not stressed. Similarly, *all right* and *already* are pronounced /uh RIT/ or /aw RIT/, with a tapped /t/, or even /uh RI?/ with a glottal stop, and /uh RE dee/, with a tapped /d/: *all right already* /uh RI duh RE dee/.

e. **The glottal stop /?/ and /t/:** In the Bronx, a glottal stop (phonetic symbol: /?/) is often heard replacing /t/ in the middle and at the end of a word: *bottle* becomes /BA ?l/. *What* is pronounced /WA?/. In New York City Hispanic-American accents, the /t/ is sometimes simply dropped before another consonant (no glottal stop replaces it), so *What does it mean?* is pronounced /WA dus ih? MEEN/. A glottal stop may substitute for the /t/ in *it*. Sometimes the final /t/ is dropped altogether, especially before another consonant: *I didn't know* /I DIH dih (alternatively, DIH ?ih) NOH/. This alternative pronunciation of *didn't* is sometimes heard in a New York City Hispanic-American accent, and it is becoming usual in New York accents generally. Notice the final /s/ in *does*, also a frequent phenomenon in Hispanic accents, in which the final voiced /z/ sound shifts to unvoiced /s/. This information can be useful in the Puerto Rican roles in the musical *West Side Story*.

f. **The sounds of /th / th/:** These consonants typically shift to /d/ and /t/, respectively, particularly in non-educated speech. Educated New Yorkers usually pronounce these sounds correctly.

5. **Specific and essential New York City pronunciations:** *coffee* /KAW fee/, *historic* /hih STAH (alternatively, STAW) rihk/, *long* /LAWNG/, *museum* /myooh ZEEM/, *on* /AHN/.

Intonation and Stress: The Music and Rhythm of the Accents

The intonation patterns for New York City are the same as for General American, with a drop in pitch at the end of declarative sentences, and a rise at the end of questions.

Practice Exercises

1. *The island of Manhattan is almost twelve miles long and absolutely filled with gorgeous buildings and parks and museums.*
General New York City: /thee I lihnd uv man HA?N ihz O mohst TWELV MOY uhlz LAWNGG and ab su LOO? lee FIHLD wihth GAW jihs BIHL dihnggz and PAWKS and myooh ZEEMZ/

Notes: The /d/ at the end of the word *and* is often dropped. The word *museum* is often pronounced /myooh ZEE uhm/, as in General American. The glottal stop in the words *Manhattan* and *absolutely* is typical of the Bronx; otherwise, say a regular /t/ in these words. The pronunciation of *miles* in very old-fashioned, and not often heard anymore.

2. *Forget about it.*
/fuh GE duh BOW (alternatively, BA) diht (alternatively, dih?)/

Notes: Originally New York City Italian, this pronunciation is now ubiquitous. Note the tapped /d/ in /duh/. In the pronunciation /diht/ the /t/ is very lightly pronounced.

3. *He wasn't going to do that, and he wouldn't have done it anyway. There were three guys out there the other day. They were taking a survey on East Fifty-Eighth Street off Park Avenue.*

/hee WU zihn GUH nuh DOOH da? an (alternatively, n) he WOO (alternatively, WOO?) nuh DU nih DEN ee way / the (alternatively, de) wuh tree (alternatively, *three*) GIZ owt the thee (alternatively, dee, with a tapped /d/) U thih day / thay (alternatively, day) wuh TAY kihn uh SOY vay ahn EEST FIHF tee AYT STREET awf PAWK (alternatively, PAHRK) Euh vih nooh (alternatively, A vih nyooh)/

Notes: The vowels in *do* and *wouldn't* are long. The /n/ in /zihn/ is nasalized; that is, the tongue does not complete the formation of the consonant /n/. Notice all the dropped consonants, the glottal stop, and the tapped /d/ in /DEN/. This is typical working-class speech, heard ubiquitously in all the boroughs of New York. With the glottal stops, it is a Bronx accent. A dentalized /t/ (/ts/) in the word *taking*, along with the dropped final /g/, is associated with a New York City Irish accent; with a /g/ added to the /ng/ and the initial /t/ dentalized, it could be a New York City Jewish or Long Island accent, as could also be the case with the word *guys*, if pronounced with a very short diphthong as /GAWeez/ instead of /GIZ/. The pronunciation of the word *survey* varies, and on the first syllable a strong /SOY/ sound is seldom heard anymore—instead, one hears /SUHR/ or /SUHee/; also, the vowel is almost always r-influenced. The /a/ in *avenue* is flat, almost an /e/, but is also heard with a more open sound.

4. *Didn't you hear what I said? I didn't ask you that. What do you want to do? Nothing? All right. Got to go. I'm going to go. You're finished. I'm finished. Baddabing, baddaboom. Need you ask? I'm out of here.*
/DIHN chuh (alternatively, chooh) HIH (alternatively, HIHR) WAH dI sed / I dihn ASK yooh DA? (alternatively, da, or that) / WAH duh yuh (alternatively, yooh) WAH nuh dooh (alternatively, WAH chuh WAH nuh dooh) / NUTH ihn (alternatively, NU? n) / AW (alternatively, U) RIT / GAH duh GOH / ahm GUH nuh (alternatively, UH nuh) GOH / YAW FIHN ihsht (alternatively, ihshd) / AHM FIHN ihsht / bah dah BIHNG bah dah BOOM

(alternatively, BOOHM) / NEE jooh ASK / ahm OW (alternatively, A) duh hih (with the /d/ tapped; alternatively, duh HIHuh)/

Notes:

1. If the final /r/ in *hear* is pronounced, it should only be lightly pro-nounced. A New York City Jewish pronunciation of the word *here* is /HEEuh/; New York City Irish is /HEEuh/ or /HEER/, with a very light retroflex /r/. A New York City Hispanic-American pronuncia-tion is /HEER/, with the back of the tongue slightly tensed on /r/.

2. Notice the ubiquitous tapped /d/ sounds in the syllables /dI/, /dihn/, /da/, and /duh/, and in *baddabing, baddaboom*, for instance. The /d/ in *do* could also be dentalized: /dzooh/. This is not neces-sarily true in a New York City Hispanic-American accent, where the /d/ can be articulated fairly far back, and the lips protruded to form the vowel /ooh/, with the mouth very closed, forming a nar-row opening. The New York City Italian version can be somewhat more open.

3. The expression (composed of nonsense syllables) *baddabing, badda-boom* is Italian-American and means "quick" or "just like that" or "before you knew it" or "that's it," and it has various other meanings depending on context. Other expressions, such as the Yiddish and Russian *nu*, pronounced /NOOH/ (meaning literally "well," with or without a question mark), also have multiple meanings; *nu* is heard in the speech of older Jewish generations, with a shrug of the shoulders thrown in for good measure. Notice that the /a/ in *ask* is long, a characteristic of some New York City Italian speakers. Watch DVDs of the HBO television series *The Sopranos* (1999–2007) for some authentic examples; although the show is set in northern New Jersey, the Italian-American accents are very much the same in the two regions.

Monologues

1. From Lanford Wilson's *Balm in Gilead* (1965)

In an all-night coffee shop on upper Broadway in Manhattan, we meet "the riffraff, the bums, the petty thieves, the scum, the lost, the desperate, the dispossessed, the cool; depending on one's attitude there are a hundred names that could describe them." The longtime heroin addict Fick describes to Tig, a male prostitute, what it was like to be mugged.

> FICK: (*They sit quietly, looking up out toward the street.*) I mean, I was just walking down the street and they came up on me like they was important, and they start pushing me around, you know. And they pushed me into this alley, not an alley, but this hallway and back down the end of that to this dark place at the end of the hallway and they start punching at me, and I just fell into this ball on the floor so they couldn't hurt me or nothing. But if I came down there with a couple of fighters, a couple of guys, like my friends, it wouldn't have to be you or anything, but just a couple or three guys, big guys, like walking down the street, you know. Just so they could see I got these buddies here. See I'm on *H*, I mean, I'm flying and I gotta talk man, but I'm serious now; just a few guys and they'd leave me be, maybe, because they'd think I had these buddies that looked after me, you know; 'cause I—you know—they kicked me up, if I wasn't on *H*, man, they'd be pains all through me—you know—walking down the street by myself—I start looking around and wondering who's out there gonna mess me up, you know.

2. From Leonard Melfi's One-Act Play *Birdbath* (1965)

Velma, who has a job clearing off the tables in a midtown Manhattan cafeteria, is from the Bronx, where she lives with her domineering mother. Although she appears innocent enough, earlier in the day she stabbed her mother to death.

VELMA: Well, I used to be real skinny, you know what I mean? I used to be all bones, almost like one of them skeletons. But since I been workin' here for Mr. Quincy, well, I've been puttin' on some weight. (*She pauses.*) That's why, in a way, this job isn't really that bad—because of the free meal they let you have. My mother said to me, "Velma, you take advantage of that free meal. You eat as much as you can . . . when something's free you make use of it . . . take as much as they let you have." And so, I've been eating pretty good lately, and Mr. Quincy, he's a nice man, he never tells me that I'm eating too much. In fact, I think he's a real nice man, because he hired me without my having any experience at all. This is the first time I've ever had a job where I cleaned off the tables and everything when the people were through eating. Boy, at first I was real scared about this job. I didn't think I was gonna be able to do it right . . . you know?

8
Canadian Accents: English, French

Teach Yourself Canadian English Accents

Canadian English accents are much the same all over the country except for Newfoundland, which has its own variations. For instance, there is an intrusive /r/ in such words as *washing* /WAWR shihng/, a pronunciation not usually heard in the rest of Canada. Called Central / Prairie Canadian English, or sometimes West-Central Canadian English, this clear and well-articulated accent is similar to Midwestern American accents, but differs from them in a few important ways.

For an example of good clear Canadian English diction, listen to Alex Trebek, the host of the American television quiz show *Jeopardy* (1984–). The television series *The Kids in the Hall* (1988–1994), available on DVD, features a group of young Canadian actors—Dave Foley, Bruce McCulloch, Kevin McDonald, Mark McKinney, and Scott Thompson—in satirical sketches.

Donald Sutherland, whom you can see in such films as *Ordinary People* (1980) and *Eye of the Needle* (1981), has superb Canadian English diction. His son, Kiefer Sutherland, who also has very fine speech, spent much of his youth in Toronto. You can hear him in *Flatliners* (1990) and *A Few Good Men* (1992). Michael J. Fox, the star of the television series *Spin City* (1996–2002) and of the *Back to the Future* film series (1985, 1989, 1990), is from Edmonton. Brendan Fraser, whose diction is impeccable, stars in such films as *With Honors* (1991), *Gods and Monsters* (1998), and *School Ties* (1992); he was born in Indianapolis but grew up partly in Canada. Listen to Hume Cronyn for some of the best and clearest diction you will ever hear, in *Lifeboat* (1944) and *Cocoon* (1985). Among other prominent actors of Canadian origin, all of whom speak beautifully, are Colleen Dewhurst (*Annie Hall*, 1977); Walter Pidgeon, always greatly dignified in his dozens of films, including *Funny Girl* (1968), in which he played Florenz Ziegfeld; Raymond Massey (*Abe Lincoln in Illinois*, 1940, and many other films); Leslie Nielsen (hilarious comedies, including *The Naked Gun*, 1988); the inimitable Walter Huston (*Yankee Doodle Dandy*, 1942, and *The Treasure of the Sierra Madre*, 1948); William Shatner (Captain Kirk in the original *Star Trek* television series, 1966–1969, and several spinoff theatrical features); Raymond Burr (who played the title role in the original *Perry Mason* television series, 1957–1966); Lorne Greene (star of the television series *Bonanza*, 1959–1973); and Patrick J. Adams, from Toronto, in the TV series *Suits* (2012–). To this list you can add the versatile and brilliant Christopher Plummer (who can sound British or American at will), Margot Kidder, Pamela Anderson, Joseph Wiseman, Dan Aykroyd, John Candy, Jim Carrey, Rick Moranis, Martin Short, Mike Myers, Catherine O'Hara, Jennifer Tilly, Meg Tilly, and Neve Campbell. Mary Pickford, "America's Sweetheart," known mostly for her silent films, was Canadian, as was Yvonne De Carlo, whose career in films spanned fifty years; see her in *For Whom the Bell Tolls* (1943) and *The Captain's Paradise* (1953).

To people who do not know that these actors are from Canada, they sound like Americans with exceptionally fine speech and clear diction. Absent from the accents of most of the people listed above is the famous Canadian pronunciation of the diphthong /ow/ as /oh/ in such words as *out*, *about*, and *house*.

1. **Positioning, placement, and use of the muscles of the mouth during speech:** The position of the vocal apparatus is much the same as for the accents of the American Midwestern states, particularly

northern Wisconsin and Minnesota, where the jaw is somewhat tighter and the lips a bit more closed and drawn a bit more to the side than in General American.

2. **The sound of /r/:** Canadian English is rhotic, with a retroflex /r/ strongly or lightly pronounced, depending on the speaker: the tongue is curled upward, its bottom toward the roof of the mouth as the consonant is articulated.

3. **Vowels and diphthongs:** In general, Canadians use the same vowel system as that of General American. Vowels tend to be short, and there are some specific phenomena to bear in mind:

    a. **The sound of /aw/:** Close to the /ah/ sound heard in Midwestern American accents, this vowel shifts to /o/, as in British RP *not*. *Law* and *saw* are pronounced /LO/ and /SO/. *Thought* and *taught* are pronounced /THOT/ and /TOT/.

    b. **The sound of /e/:** In an unstressed syllable before an /r/, /e/ often shifts to a schwa /uh/. For example, the word *there*, when not stressed, becomes /thuhr/. On the other hand, *bury* is usually pronounced /BE ree/, but *strawberry* is usually pronounced /STRO bree/.

    c. **The sound of /I/:** Although usually pronounced /I/, this diphthong sometimes shifts to /UHee/, especially in rural speech.

    d. **The sound of /o/:** In such words as *horrible*, *hot*, *got*, *not*, and *ponder*, the short /o/ used in British RP is heard, as opposed to the /ah/ of General American.

    e. **The sound of /ow/:** This is the stereotypical Canadian sound that Americans always notice, even though not all Canadians say it this way. Before a voiceless consonant or when it is the end of a word, instead of saying /Aooh/, as in General American, the Canadian says /OH/, so *about* is pronounced /uh BOHT/ and *house* is /HOHS/. However, before a voiced consonant, this diphthong is pronounced /ow/, in such words as *brown*, *cloud*, and *clown*.

f. **The sound of /w/:** Words spelled with "wh" are pronounced with /hw/: *white* /HWUHeeT/ in Toronto and in Ontario generally, but not in the Western Provinces, where "wh" is pronounced /w/, in the same way as in General American.

g. **The sound of /yooh/:** The /y/ is usually not pronounced in words like *news* and *duke*. Canadians say /NOOHZ/ and /DOOHK/.

4. **Other consonants:** The consonants are very strong and well articulated.

a. **The sound of /l/:** The Canadian /l/ is pronounced with the blade of the tongue slightly forward and pressed to the roof of the mouth, whereas for the General American /l/ you have to drop the blade of the tongue slightly.

b. **The sound of /t/:** The /t/ is sometimes strongly aspirated at the end of a word, and even sometimes in the middle of a word.

5. **Three Canadian pronunciations:** *Khaki* /KAHR kee/; *bilingual* /bI LIHN gyooh uhl/. The past participle *been* usually rhymes with *bean*, as in British RP, but may also sometimes rhyme with *bin*.

Intonation and Stress: The Music and Rhythm of the Accents

Intonation and stress are the same as for General American. See chapter 1 for details.

Practice Exercises

1. *How now, brown cow?*
/HOW NOH BROWN KOH/

2. *Finish what you're doing and come outside. We don't have all day, you know. We're about to leave for a long time. Anyway, it's too hot out there.*
/FIHN eesh WU chuhr DOOH eeng an KUM oht SID / wee dohnt hav AHL day yuh NOH / wihuh ruh BOH tuh LEEV fruh LONG TIM / E nee way its tooh HO doht THER/

Notes: Notice the diphthongization of the word *we're*. The /d/ in the syllable /doht/ is tapped.

3. *We had a wonderful hot meal there, and it was so delicious we could hardly eat it all.*
/wee had uh WUN duhr fuhl MEEuhL THER and iht wuhz soh dih LIH shuhs wee kood HAHRD lee EE dih DAHL/

4. *That about completes our survey of Canadian English, eh?*
/that uh BOHT kum PLEETS AHR SUHR vay uhv kuh NAY dee uhn IHNG glihsh AY/

Note: The /d/ in *Canadian* may either be tapped or strongly articulated.

Monologues
1. From John McLachlan Gray's (with Eric Peterson) *Billy Bishop Goes to War* (1978), Act 1
This play with music is set during World War II. Young Billy Bishop tells of his experiences.

> BISHOP: I could ride a horse. And I was a good shot. I mean, I am a really good shot. I've got these tremendous eyes, you see. And Royal Military College had an entrance exam—which was good because my previous scholastic record wasn't that hot. In fact, when I told my principal that indeed I was going to RMC, he said, "Bishop, you don't have the brains." But I studied real hard, sat for the exams, and got in.
> *The PIANO PLAYER beats a military snare-drum pattern on his knees.*
> BISHOP: (*as officer*) Recruits! Recruits will march at all times, they will not loiter, they will not window-shop. Recruits! Recruits will be soundly trounced every Friday night, whether they deserve it

or not! (*as himself*) I mean those guys were nuts! They were going to make leaders out of us—the theory being that before you
could lead, you had to learn to obey. So because of this we were
all assigned to an upperclassman as a kind of, well, slave. And
I got assigned to this real sadistic SOB, this guy named Vivian
Bishop—that's right, it's the same surname as me, and because
of this, I had to tuck him in at night, kiss him on the forehead,
and say, "Goodnight, sir!"

2. From Kelly Rebar's *Bordertown Café* (1987), Act 1

The play is set in "a café on the Alberta-Montana border," so we meet
Americans as well as Canadians. Marlene is one of the Canadians in
this story about dysfunctional families. This is her reply when Jimmy,
who has come up to the café from Montana, tells her he wants nothing
from her.

MARLENE: Yes, you do. You want something I just don't have.
And never will. When I got somethin' to say, I *can't* just say it to
you. I'm not her. I'm not the kinda wife your dad needed. I'm not
my mother, I'm not Aunt Thelma, I'm no one—just myself. I got
a few dollars in the Bank o' Montreal, I got a car, I'm thirty-four
years old with fallen arches and a sore back. But you know what?
I *like* this place. And any changes I make I wanna make in my own
good time. But first, I'm gonna . . . tra-vel.
　　Pause
[JIMMY: *Travel?*
JIM: Travel?]
MARLENE: Booked my flight today. To Hawaii. And I'm goin'.
Come Christmas. Two weeks accommodation. Wardair. You said
I needed a holiday. Well, I'm takin' one.

Teach Yourself Canadian French Accents

Canadian French differs considerably from the French spoken in France. There are a number of Canadian French accents in French, among them the accent of Québec City, the accent of Montreal, and the rural accents of Québec Province. The accents in English vary accordingly. To do an authentic accent, learn some French, and learn to pronounce it with a Québecois accent.

Among French Canadian actors who provide great lessons in doing a light accent are François Arnaud as Cesare Borgia in the television series *The Borgias* (2011–); and Lothaire Bluteau in *Black Robe* (1991) and *I Shot Andy Warhol* (1996); hear Bluteau also in *Jesus of Montreal* (1989), in Québecois French. Geneviève Bujold, in such films as *Anne of the Thousand Days* (1969) and *Dead Ringers* (1989), has almost no French accent, except perhaps for the softness of her consonants.

1. **Positioning, placement, and use of the muscles of the mouth during speech:** In Canadian French, the jaw is a bit looser and lower than in the French of France, which makes a Canadian French accent different immediately from that of Europe. During speech, the muscles at the corner of the mouth are slightly tensed during speech, and the tongue is held slightly down and forward, with the lips slightly protruded. This basic position carries over into an accent in English.

2. **The sounds of /r/:** In Montreal, the /r/ is often trilled or given one light tap. In the city of Québec, the uvular /r/ is used; it is also sometimes heard in Montreal. Either /r/ can carry over into English. The correct retroflex /r/ is often learned, but pronounced with the back of the tongue slightly tensed and the lips protruded.

3. **Vowels and diphthongs:** The vowel system of Canadian French does not differ markedly from that of the French of France, except that nasal vowels are often diphthongized, and /ah/ often shifts to

/aw/. English vowels and diphthongs are usually learned correctly, with the following exceptions:

   a. **The shift from /ih/ to /ee/:** The vowel /ih/ in *bit* does not exist in French, and /ee/ is often substituted for it in a heavy accent: *I think it's true* /I teenk eets TROOH/.

   b. **The sound of /u/:** The vowel /u/ in *but* does not exist in French, and is often pronounced /ah/: *But it's up above* /baht eets ahp uh (alternatively, ah) BAHV/.

4. **Other consonants:** Consonants can be softer than in General American, but are otherwise the same. In Québec, but not in Montreal, /d/ and /t/ are pronounced /dz/ and /ts/ in French, but this does not carry over into an accent in English.

   a. **Dropping of initial /h/:** In French, "h" is only used in orthography, and a link is made with a preceding word: *très habile* /tre zah BEEL/ (very clever). In some words a link is not made between /h/ and a preceding word, and this /h/ is called an "aspirated /h/": *haricot* /ah ree KO/ (bean) is such a word; *les haricots* /lé ah ree KO/ (the beans) is never pronounced /lé zah ree KO/. In Québécois, the aspirated /h/ is sometimes pronounced: /hah ree KO/. So French Canadians often learn to pronounce initial /h/, but in an accent in English /h/ is nevertheless frequently dropped: *him* /IHM/. /H/ is sometimes inserted where it is silent in English: *hour* /HOW uhr/ instead of /OW uhr/.

   b. **The sounds of /th / *th*/:** These sounds do not exist in French. French Canadians who have not learned to pronounce them correctly usually substitute /d/ and /t/ for the voiced /th/ and the voiceless /*th*/, respectively. For a light accent, do the correct versions.

   c. **Consonant cluster reduction:** In consonant clusters, certain sounds are dropped. In words like *picture* and *edge* the /t/ and /d/ are dropped: /PIHK shuhr/, /EZH/, *on the edge* /awn duh EZH/. Since /j/ doesn't exist in French, in a French Canadian accent /j/

is heard as /zh/. The final /d/ in such words as *hold* and the /t/ in such words as *fast* are dropped.

Intonation and Stress: The Music and Rhythm of the Accents

The most important feature of a French accent in English is the stress pattern carried over from the French language. In English, every word is individually stressed. But French is spoken in "rhythmic phrases," also called "stress groups" or "breath groups." French communicates ideas by means of these rhythmic phrases rather than by stressing individual words.

Because any French Canadian learning English knows that rhythmic phrasing is not correct, there is usually an attempt to compensate for the stressing by making both syllables fairly even, as if there were a slight confusion as to which syllable should be stressed, or by stressing an incorrect syllable; see practice exercises 3 and 4.

A rhythmic phrase may consist of only one word, such as *Arrêtez!* /ah re TÉ/ (Stop!), but it usually consists of a group of words that form a logical grammatical entity, such as a noun with its adjectives or a verb with a pronoun subject and an adverb. The last syllable of the group is stressed, except for syllables containing a schwa /uh/, called an *e muet* /uh mü É/ (mute e) in French. For example, in the phrase *la table* /lah TAH bluh/ (the table), the syllable /TAH/ is stressed because the last syllable contains a schwa.

Stress in a French word changes depending on the position of the word in a rhythmic phrase. For example, in the phrase *la maison* /lah mé ZON/ (the house) the last syllable is stressed; the /n/ is nasal. If we add an adjective to the phrase and make it *la maison blanche* /lah mé zon BLAHN shuh/ (the white house), the stress shifts to the first syllable of the word for *white*. The schwa in the last syllable of *blanche* is usually silent in ordinary speech: /BLAHNSH/.

Practice Exercises

1. *Je peux le dire.*

Québecois: /zhuh PO luh DZEE uhr/ or even /zhuh po LDZEE uhr/
Standard French: /zhuh po luh DEER/ or even /zhuh po LDEER/

                    di-\

                         ire.

          peux

     Je   le

Translation: I can say it.

Notes: In this Québecois intonation pattern, note the falling tone, indicated by the backward slash, on *dire*, diphthongized in a Canadian French accent. There is secondary stressing on the word *peux* (can) in both accents, but in Québecois, the vowel is longer and the stress stronger.

2. *I'm going to tell you, that's right, me, I'm going to make it plain to you what I think. By gar, if that's the way you want it that's the way it's going to be.*
/ahm GAW nuh tel YOOH \\ das rIt \\ mee \\ ahm GAW nuh mek eet plen too YOOH \\ wah dI TEENK \\ bI GAHR \\ eef dats duh WAY yooh wawn eet \\ dats duh way eets GAW nuh bee\\ /

Notes: The stress group endings, indicated by the two backward slashes following them, are quite strong. The expression *by gar* (by God) is an old clichéd version of a Canadian French accent. It's what French trappers say in such forgotten novels as Robert W. Chambers's *The Little Red Foot* (George F. Doran Company, 1921), a story that takes place in Upstate New York during the American Revolution.

3. *Even while being concerned for my safety, I rescued the drowning sailor.*
/EE VEN wil BE IHNG KON SORND faw mI SAYF TEE I RES KYOOHD duh DROW NIHNG SAY LUHR/

Note: This is practice for the overcompensatory stress patterns that sometimes are heard in this accent.

4. I regard him as admirable. It's too much, I tell you, just too much, don't you think? The elections are going to be held whether they want them to be or not. Our voices will be heard!

/I REE gahrd IHM az ad MEE rah buhl / ees tooh MOSH ah tel yooh jos (alternatively, zhos) tooh MOSH dohn yooh TIHNK / dee ih LEK shuhnz ahr GAW nuh bee ELD WE DUHR day wawn uhm tooh bee awr NOT / ahr VOY seez weel (alternatively, wihl) be ORD (alternatively, HERD, or HORD)/

Note: Do a standard retroflex /r/ with the lips slightly protruded and the back of the tongue slightly tensed, or a uvular or trilled /r/ for a really heavy accent.

A Scene for Three and a Monologue

1. From David Fennario's *Balconville* (1979), Act 1, Scene 2

Set in the Pointe-Saint-Charles district of Montreal, this play takes as its background the separatist movement that wants Québec to secede from Canada. In this story of complicated relationships between French-speaking and Anglophone neighbors, many of the characters speak Québecois as well as English. The following brief scene features Cécile, who usually speaks French, talking with Muriel and Johnny. Cécile has come out onto the balcony of her apartment building with breadcrumbs to feed to the birds, and she throws some down just as Muriel "comes out of her house carrying a basket of washing."

> MURIEL: Jesus Murphy!
> CÉCILE: Oh, excuse me, madame. Excuse me. Hello.
> MURIEL: Yeah, hello . . .

CÉCILE: Aw, it's so nice, eh?

MURIEL: What?

CÉCILE: The sun. It's so nice.

MURIEL: Yeah, I guess it is.

CÉCILE: It's so good for my plants.

JOHNNY: How are your tomatoes?

CÉCILE: My tomatoes? Very good. This year, I think I get some big ones. Last year, I don't know what happened to them.

JOHNNY: The cat pissed on them.

CÉCILE: The what?

JOHNNY: The big tomcat that's always hanging around with Muriel. He pissed on them.

CÉCILE: You think so?

JOHNNY: Sure.

2. From Tomson Highway's *Dry Lips Oughta Move to Kapuskasing* (1989), Act 1

Kapuskasing, a center of the timber industry, is a town on the river of the same name in northern Ontario. The play is set on a nearby Native reservation. Pierre St. Pierre talks to Dickie Bird Halked /HAHL ked/, whose paternity is uncertain. Pierre's accent should not be too heavy. Do a retroflex /r/, not a guttural or trilled /r/. But do shift /th/ to /d/ and /*th*/ to /t/. Drop the initial /h/ sounds. And do some rhythmic phrasing.

PIERRE: (*Now alone with DICKIE BIRD, half-whispering to him. As PIERRE speaks, DICKIE BIRD again takes the crucifix off the wall and returns with it to his seat, taking the booties off in haphazard fashion.*) Has he been feedin' you this crappola, too? Don't you be startin' that foolishness. That Spooky Lacroix's so fulla shit he wouldn't know a two-thousand-year-old Egyptian Sphinxter if he came face to face with one. He's just preachifyin' at you because you're the one person on this reserve who can't argue back. You listen to me. I was there in the same room as your mother when she gave birth to you. So I know well who you are and where you come from. I remember the whole picture. Even though we are all in a bit of a fizzy . . . I remember. Do you know, Dickie Bird Halked, that you were named after that bar? Anyone ever tell you that?

SELECTED BIBLIOGRAPHY

Accents Resources

Barber, Charles. *The English Language: A Historical Introduction*. Edinburgh: The Edinburgh University Press, 1997.

Baugh, John. *Black Street Speech*. Austin: University of Texas Press, 1983.

Blumenfeld, Robert. *Accents: A Manual for Actors*. Revised and Expanded Edition. New York: Limelight Editions, 2002.

Brook, G. I. *Varieties of English*. London: MacMillan and St. Martin's Press, 1973.

Bryson, Bill. *Made in America: An Informal History of the English Language in the United States*. New York: Avon Books, 1990.

Comrie, Bernard, ed. *The World's Major Languages*. New York: Oxford University Press, 1990.

Cruttenden, Alan. *Intonation*. New York: Cambridge University Press, 1986.

Crystal, David. *The Cambridge Encyclopedia of the English Language*. New York: Cambridge University Press, 1995.

Dillard, J. L. *Black English: Its History and Usage in the United States*. New York: Vintage Books, 1973.

Giegerich, Heinz J. *English Phonology*. New York: Cambridge University Press, 1992.

Gimson's Pronunciation of English. 5th edition, revised by Alan Cruttenden. London: Edward Arnold, 1994.

Holloway, Joseph E., and Winifred K. Vass. *The African Heritage of American English*. Indianapolis: Indiana University Press, 1997.

Jones, Daniel. *An English Pronouncing Dictionary*. 15th edition. Edited by Peter Roach and James Hartman. New York: Cambridge University Press, 1997.

———. *The Pronunciation of English*. New York: Cambridge University Press, 1992.

Ladefoged, Peter. *A Course in Phonetics*. 3rd edition. Philadelphia: Harcourt, Brace College Publishers, 1993.

———, and Ian Maddieson. *The Sounds of the World's Languages*. Oxford: Blackwell Publishers, 1996.

McArthur, Tom, ed. *The Oxford Companion to the English Language*. New York: Oxford University Press, 1992.

McCrum, Robert, William Cran, and Robert MacNeil. *The Story of English* (a companion to the PBS series). New York: Elizabeth Sifton Books, Viking, 1986.

Mencken, H. L. *The American Language: An Inquiry into the Development of the English Language in the United States* (together with its two supplements). New York: Alfred A. Knopf, 1936.

Schneider, Edgar W., ed. *Varieties of English 2: The Americas and the Caribbean*. Berlin: Mouton de Gruyter, 2008.

Skinner, Edith. *Speak with Distinction*. Revised with new material added by Timothy Monich and Lilene Mansell. Edited by Lilene Mansell. New York: Applause, 1990.

Wells, J. C. *Accents of English*, in three volumes: (1) *Introduction*; (2) *The British Isles*; (3) *Beyond the British Isles*. New York: Cambridge University Press, 1992.

———. *English Intonation: An Introduction*. New York: Cambridge University Press, 2006.

Wolfram, Walt, and Natalie Schilling-Estes. *Hoi Toide on the Outer Banks: The Story of the Ocracoke Brogue*. Chapel Hill: The University of North Carolina Press, 1997.

Literary Sources

Alcott, Louisa May. *Little Men: Life at Plumfield with Jo's Boys*. Project Gutenberg electronic edition, 2008.

Childress, Alice. *Wine in the Wilderness*. New York: Dramatists Play Service. 1969.

Cruz, Nilo. *Hortensia and the Museum of Dreams*. In *Two Sisters and a Piano and Other Plays* by Nilo Cruz. New York: Theatre Communications Group, 2007.

Eisenberg, Deborah. *Pastorale*. Excerpted in *The Actor's Book of Contemporary Stage Monologues*, edited by Nina Shengold. New York: Penguin Books, 1987.

Fennario, David. *Balconville*. In *Modern Canadian Plays*, volume 1, 5th edition, edited by Jerry Wasserman. Vancouver, Canada: Talonbooks, 2012.

Gibbons, Rawle. *Ten to One*. In *A Calypso Trilogy* by Rawle Gibbons. Kingston, Jamaica: Ian Randle Publishers, 1999.

Gray, John MacLachlan, with Eric Peterson. *Billy Bishop Goes to War*. In *Modern Canadian Plays*, volume 1, 5th edition, edited by Jerry Wasserman. Vancouver, Canada: Talonbooks, 2012.

Hansberry, Lorraine. *A Raisin in the Sun*. New York: Signet, 1966.

Henley, Beth. *Crimes of the Heart*. Excerpted in *The Actor's Book of Contemporary Stage Monologues*, edited by Nina Shengold. New York: Penguin Books, 1987.

Highway, Tomson. *Dry Lips Oughta Move to Kapuskasing*. In *Modern Canadian Plays*, volume 1, 5th edition, edited by Jerry Wasserman. Vancouver, Canada: Talonbooks, 2012.

Hippolyte, Kendel. *The Drum-Maker: A Play in Three Movements*. In *Caribbean Plays for Playing*, edited by Keith Noel. Portsmouth, NH: Heinemann Educational Books, 1985.

Howe, Tina. *The Art of Dining*. New York: Samuel French, 1987.

———. *Painting Churches*. Excerpted in *The Actor's Book of Contemporary Stage Monologues*, edited by Nina Shengold. New York: Penguin Books, 1987.

Kramer, Larry. *The Normal Heart*. New York: Grove Press, 2000.

Mamet, David. *Glengarry Glen Ross: A Play*. New York: Samuel French, 1983.

———. *Sexual Perversity in Chicago*. In *Sexual Perversity in Chicago and The Duck Variations: Two Comedies*. New York: Samuel French, 2010.

Mann, Emily. *Still Life*. New York: Dramatists Play Service, 1982.

Melfi, Leonard. *Birdbath*. In *Encounters: Six One-Act Plays* by Leonard Melfi. New York: Samuel French, 1995.

O'Neill, Eugene. *Long Day's Journey Into Night*. New Haven, CT: Yale University Press, 1956.

Piñero, Miguel. *Short Eyes*. New York: Hill and Wang, 1975.

Rebar, Kelly. *Bordertown Café*. In *Modern Canadian Plays*, volume 1, 5th edition, edited by Jerry Wasserman. Vancouver, Canada: Talonbooks, 2012.

Rivera, José. *Cloud Tectonics*. In *Marisol and Other Plays* by José Rivera. New York: Theatre Communications Group, 1997.

Scott, Dennis. *The Crime of Annabel Campbell*. In *Caribbean Plays for Playing*, edited by Keith Noel. Portsmouth, NH: Heinemann Educational Books, 1985.

Tolan, Kathleen. *A Weekend Near Madison*. New York: Samuel French, 1984.

Twain, Mark. *The Adventures of Tom Sawyer*. Project Gutenberg electronic edition, 2006.

Valdez, Luis. *Bandido!* In *Zoot Suit and Other Plays* by Luis Valdez. Houston, TX: Arte Público Press, 1992.

Walcott, Derek. *Dream on Monkey Mountain*. In *Dream on Monkey Mountain and Other Plays* by Derek Walcott. New York: Farrar, Straus and Giroux, 1971.

Williams, Matt. *Between Daylight and Boonville*. New York: Samuel French, 1983.

Williams, Tennessee. *Cat on a Hot Tin Roof*. In *Tennessee Williams: Eight Plays*. New York: Nelson Doubleday, 1979.

———. *Orpheus Descending*. In *Tennessee Williams: Eight Plays*. New York: Nelson Doubleday, 1979.

———. *Small Craft Warnings*. New York: New Directions, 1972.

———. *A Streetcar Named Desire*. In *Tennessee Williams: Eight Plays*. New York: Nelson Doubleday, 1979.

———. *Vieux Carré*. New York: New Directions, 1979.

Wilson, August. *Ma Rainey's Black Bottom*. New York: Penguin, 1985.

Wilson, Lanford. *Balm in Gilead*. In *Lanford Wilson: Collected Works, 1965–1970*. Portland, ME: Smith and Kraus, 1996.

ABOUT THE AUTHOR

Robert Blumenfeld is the author of *Accents: A Manual for Actors* (1998; Revised and Expanded Edition, 2002); *Acting with the Voice: The Art of Recording Books* (2004); *Tools and Techniques for Character Interpretation: A Handbook of Psychology for Actors, Writers, and Directors* (2006); *Using the Stanislavsky System: A Practical Guide to Character Creation and Period Styles* (2008); *Blumenfeld's Dictionary of Acting and Show Business* (2009); *Blumenfeld's Dictionary of Musical Theater: Opera, Operetta, Musical Comedy* (2010); *Stagecraft: Stanislavsky and External Acting Technique--A Companion to Using the Stanislavsky System* (2011); *Teach Yourself Accents--The British Isles: A Handbook for Young Actors and Speakers* (2013); and the collaborator with noted teacher, acting coach, and actress Alice Spivak on the writing of her book *How to Rehearse When There Is No Rehearsal: Acting and the Media* (2007)--all published by Limelight. He lives and works as an actor, dialect coach, and writer in New York City, and is a longtime member of Equity, AFTRA, and SAG. He has worked in numerous regional and New York theaters, as well as in television and independent films, and performed in many comedies and farces. For ACT Seattle he played the title role in Ronald Harwood's *The Dresser*, and he has performed many roles in plays by Shakespeare and Chekhov, as well as doing an Off-Broadway season of six Gilbert and Sullivan comic operas for Dorothy Raedler's American Savoyards (under the name Robert Fields), for which he played the Lord Chancellor in *Iolanthe* and other patter-song roles. In 1994, he performed in Michael John LaChiusa's musical *The Petrified Prince*, directed by Harold Prince at the New York Shakespeare Festival's Public Theater. For the Mc-Carter Theatre in Princeton, New Jersey, Mr. Blumenfeld performed the role of the First Voice in Dylan Thomas's *Under Milk Wood*.

He created the roles of the Marquis of Queensberry and two prosecuting attorneys in Moisés Kaufman's Off-Broadway hit play *Gross Indecency: The Three Trials of Oscar Wilde*, and was also the production's dialect coach, a job that he did as well for the Broadway musicals *Saturday Night Fever* and *The Scarlet Pimpernel* (third version and national tour) and for the New York workshop of David Henry Hwang's rewritten version of Rodgers and Hammerstein's *Flower Drum Song*. At the Manhattan School of Music, he was dialect coach for Dona D. Vaughn's production of Strauss's *Die Fledermaus* (2009) and for Jay Lesenger's production of Weill's *Street Scene* (2008), which he also coached for Mr. Lesenger at the Chautauqua Opera. Mr. Blumenfeld currently records books for Audible, among them *Pale Fire* and *Bend Sinister* by Vladimir Nabokov and *A Modest Proposal* by Jonathan Swift. He has recorded more than 320 Talking Books for the American Foundation for the Blind, including the complete Sherlock Holmes canon (four novels and fifty-six short stories), Victor Hugo's *The Hunchback of Notre-Dame*, Alexandre Dumas's *The Count of Monte Cristo*, a bilingual edition of Rainer Maria Rilke's previously unpublished poetry, and a bilingual edition of Samuel Beckett's *Waiting for Godot*, which he recorded in Beckett's original French and the playwright's own English translation. He received the 1997 Canadian National Institute for the Blind's Torgi Award for the Talking Book of the Year in the Fiction category, for his recording of Pat Conroy's *Beach Music*; and the 1999 Alexander Scourby Talking Book Narrator of the Year Award in the Fiction category.

He holds a B.A. in French from Rutgers University and an M.A. from Columbia University in French Language and Literature. Mr. Blumenfeld speaks French, German, and Italian fluently, and has smatterings of Russian, Spanish, and Yiddish.

CD TRACK LISTING

Tracks 2 through 9 contain the Practice Exercises for each chapter. Track 2 also includes the Ask List (p. 19).